BELIEF AND BELONGING

BELIEF AND BELONGING
Living and Celebrating the Faith

From the French Text
Livre de la Foi
by the
Bishops of Belgium

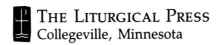

THE LITURGICAL PRESS
Collegeville, Minnesota

NIHIL OBSTAT ROBERT C. HARREN *Censor deputatus*

IMPRIMATUR ✝ JEROME HANUS, O.S.B.
       Bishop of St. Cloud

DATE DECEMBER 7, 1989

COVER DESIGN: Don Bruno
BOOK DESIGN AND LAYOUT: Don Molloy

Translation from the French text written by the Bishops of Belgium. Original title: *Livre de la Foi,* published jointly by Desclée and Novalis, 1987. © 1987 Conférence épiscopale de Belgique, Bruxelles.

Scripture quotations are from the *New American Bible with Revised New Testament,* © 1986 Confraternity of Christian Doctrine. The text of the Old Testament in *The New American Bible with Revised New Testament* was published in *The New American Bible,* © 1970 Confraternity of Christian Doctrine. Other quotations, as indicated, are from *The Jerusalem Bible,* © 1966 by Darton, Longman & Todd, Ltd. and Doubleday & Company, Inc.

Library of Congress Cataloging-in-Publication Data

Livre de la foi. English.
    Belief and belonging : living and celebrating the faith : from the French text Livre de la foi / by the bishops of Belgium.
        p.   cm.
    ISBN 0-8146-1598-8
    1. Catholic Church—Doctrines. 2. Catholic Church—Catechisms.
I. Title.
BX1751.2.L5413   1990
230'.2—dc20   90-35750
                                                                    CIP

ISBN 0-8146-1598-8

Contents

Part I

Part II

Celebrating the Lord 71

Part III

Living the Gospel 147

Index of Prayers

Photo Credits

All photographs Copyright © 1990 by the photographers.

S. N. Bauer: pp. 72, 87.
S. N. Bauer / St. Cloud Visitor: pp. 134, 157, 197 (bottom).
S. Annette Brophy: pp. 27, 57, 58, 82 (top), 96, 136, 145, 165, 171, 208, 216 (l.), 217 (bottom).
Catholic News Service: p. 97 (Carolyn A. McKeone), p. 123 bottom (Susan McKinney).
CLEO: pp. 30, 31, 43, 59, 64, 107 (bottom), 108, 131, 151, 176, 206.
Alan Cliburn: pp. 75, 94, 126, 127, 128 (bottom), 177, 182.
Vivienne della Grotta: pp. 26, 29, 53, 129, 209, 210.
Gail Denham: pp. 7, 10, 18 (bottom), 47, 55, 107 (top), 113, 114, 128 (top), 155, 172, 175, 178, 179 (top), 197 (top), 211, 217 (top r.).
Joseph A. DiChello Jr.: pp. 3, 25, 34, 36, 48, 69, 71, 77, 82 (bottom), 85, 180, 183, 202, 216 (r.).
Jeffrey High / Image Productions: pp. 2, 16, 38, 49, 120, 122 (r.), 179 (bottom), 189, 212, 220.
Sue Illg / St. Cloud Visitor: p. 140.
Joseph M. Mejuto: pp. 100, 122 (l.), 143, 193, 198 (top), 204.
Roger W. Neal: pp. 9, 63, 99, 116, 119, 147, 158, 218.
Photo Agora: Dale Gehman, p. 80; D. Michael Hostetler, p. 42; Ken Layman, p. 15; Jim King, pp. 214, 219; Robert Maust, pp. 5, 41, 65, 76, 78, 98, 103, 185 (both), 205; Marilyn Nolt, p. 187; Howard Zehr, pp. 19, 62.
Will and Angie Rumpf: p. 192.
Springlife Studios: Cover and pp. 1, 11, 13, 54, 67, 91, 104, 105, 110, 123 (top), 141, 159, 168, 184, 194, 196, 207, 217 (top l.).
Sunrise / Trinity Photos: pp. 38, 52, 79, 81, 92, 109.
Bob Taylor: pp. 12, 18 (top), 44, 51, 124, 148, 174, 188 (bottom), 191.
Betty Hurwich Zoss: pp. 95, 142, 188 (top), 198 (bottom).

Foreword

Pastors speak of the desire of many of today's Catholics for a deeper understanding of their Christian faith. I have listened to many people who are looking for a clearer and challenging restatement of our teaching, for guidance and growth in prayer, and for support and encouragement in Christian service. In spite of, or perhaps because of, the difficulties facing those who claim to be faithful followers of Jesus Christ in the midst of our modern world, there is a great flowering of renewed interest in a deepened Christian commitment.

It is in this context, and in the hope of feeding the Spirit-inspired hunger, that the Holy Father and many bishops have been looking toward the development of catechisms, programs for lay spiritual development, and so on. One of the truly successful efforts along these lines was prepared by the bishops of Belgium. Drawing on the creative pastoral and catechetical advances in their country over the past several decades, and grounded in the rich theological traditions that have found a home there for centuries, the Belgian bishops published a faith guide, which is now available for the first time in English. Entitled *Belief and Belonging: Living and Celebrating the Faith,* this English translation offers to us the promise of profound assistance in our growth in faith.

Belief and Belonging aims at an integrated vision of the Christian life. It contains thoughtful reflections on the fundamental truths of the faith, particularly as contained in the

Creed. It offers realistic assistance to all who seek to be faithful in prayer. It tackles the challenge of witnessing to the faith by a daily life made new in Christ.

Parents will be pleased to find sprinkled throughout the book the texts of the traditional prayers we learned to cherish as young people. They will assist families in passing along these important vessels of faithfulness. The very readable message of *Belief and Belonging,* designed to promote a deeper understanding, is written in narrative style, with reference questions and topic headings lining the margins for easy reference.

"Believers cannot be silent about this faith that sustains them" (Part I). But neither can believers speak their faith meaningfully unless they have taken the time to reflect on it, both individually and with others, and have found a contemporary language to communicate the Good News of Jesus Christ. The Roman Catholic bishops of Belgium have provided us with a forum for study, for reflection, and for a new articulation of our faith. I am grateful to them and to The Liturgical Press for making their work available to us in English. I recommend *Belief and Belonging* to study groups, to families, and to individuals who long for fidelity. "A Christian does not invent his or her own faith. It is received from the Church. One adheres to it by fidelity to the Apostles." *Belief and Belonging* will make a real contribution to Christian renewal.

✝ **John R. Roach**
Archbishop of Saint Paul and Minneapolis
November 14, 1989

Part I

Believing and Confessing One's Faith

The Challenge of Faith

We live in exciting times, even though the world's economic problems weigh heavily upon us on both a national and international level. Technological revolutions continue to offer completely new and unsuspected possibilities. Certain moral and social values are also better affirmed and better defended now than they were at an earlier time, even though they are not always respected. This is the case with human rights and social attainment, for example.

Our cultural environment has become quite varied, and all kinds of thought-currents coexist—some detrimental, others beneficial. Christians have contributed to humanity's social, scientific, and cultural progress, yet the question "Why are you Christian?" or "What does 'being Christian' mean for you and for others in a pluralistic society?" can still be asked. Not only do we no longer live in a homogeneous culture, but we have become "Christians in diaspora," scattered among contemporaries who do not think as we do.

In this context we are challenged by the words "Christian, acknowledge your dignity! Say who you are and in whom

"Christian, acknowledge your dignity!" (St. Leo the Great)

3

you have placed your faith." But by saying who we are we share in the faith of all those who have gone before us and of all those who, scattered throughout the world, live the same faith. Prior to being individual Christians, we have a tradition, a creed. We are a "people," a community, a Church.

Is there still the Good News?

For many of us, Christian faith offers nothing that can satisfy our daily needs. It brings neither happiness nor solutions to our problems, nor healing for our body, nor peace of mind, nor salvation, nor liberation.

Nevertheless, the healing of the total person—body, mind, and soul—is at the heart of Jesus' message. "He went around . . . proclaiming the gospel of the kingdom, and curing every disease and illness . . . . They brought to him all who were sick with various diseases and racked with pain . . . and he cured them" (Matt 4:23 ff.). Jesus healed the paralytic at the same time he forgave him his sins. Healing and pardon for sins: that is what is meant by the word *salvation*—"health" for the whole person, a deep harmony. Salvation is not limited to individuals, but reaches to all peoples and to the whole universe. Its scope includes all our relationships and all the structures of our society. Salvation depends on the message of Jesus, primarily on his life, his death, and his resurrection. Jesus, God and man, has given himself entirely for us and for all human beings "that they might have life and have it more abundantly" (John 10:10). In Jesus' resurrection all humanity is snatched from the power of death and the forces of evil. The spirit of Christ gives Christians faith, hope, and love, and that spirit is felt where God wills.

*How does one believe
or begin again to believe?*

The first stirring of faith, the first gift, the first grace, is to let go of the certitude that I will find an answer all by myself. Prayer, then, allows me to take a first step because it carries me outside of myself.

How can I believe if I build my whole life upon myself or if I depend on human powers alone? "This is the time of fulfillment. The kingdom of God is at hand. Repent, and believe in the gospel" (Mark 1:15), proclaimed Jesus. Thus he calls for conversion. To be converted is to turn toward another in order to welcome him or her.

For St. Paul, faith is the result of preaching: it "comes from what is heard, and what is heard comes through the word of Christ'' (Rom 10:17). We hear the same scriptural passages dozens of times. Yet the main thing is to grasp what God is saying to us: ''It is for you.'' It is not enough to understand; it is still necessary to be ''cut to the heart'' (Acts 2:37), like the way Peter's discourse affected the crowd on Pentecost.

The Word of God has been transmitted to us by others: by our family, by the Christian community, by men and women immersed in the Church's faith. Before we were able to read the Passion of Christ in the Gospels, somebody showed us Christ on the cross and talked with us about his death and resurrection. Before we understood we believed.

How does God speak to humans?

The Gospels reach us over a long path through the history of humanity and the Church. Missionaries came to spread the gospel in our country, and our Church has sent missionaries to bring to other peoples the Word that gives us life. In this process of evangelizing, it is the Spirit that makes hearts burn. God is thus at work in the history of men and women who, generation after generation, live and transmit the faith.

God attracts men and women: certain ones in their youth, others at an older age. He speaks to them in the beauty of nature, in the witness of believers, in the events of life, in joy or pain, and through the combat and bloodshed of the martyrs of Christ. When perhaps our mother helps us, it is the Church evangelizing us through her. Perhaps it is a stranger whose faith shows in word and deed. In all these signs God goes before us.

How can we believe when misfortune strikes us?

Like love, faith is not protected from life's misfortunes and hardships. Nor is it immune from doubt, weariness, or boredom. The testing of faith is inherent in the life of faith. It is not necessarily bound to one's condition of existence. It is not always those born in misery who refuse to believe. On the contrary, those who have been loved and have benefited from every opportunity may not have—or no longer have—faith in anyone but themselves.

When we see the immense suffering in the world, it makes us want to doubt God. To embrace a worthy faith, it is often necessary that we see it somehow at work: when it becomes Good News for the poor, then God in some way becomes "visible."

To believe is to be supported by someone.

Our profession of faith does not begin with "I believe *that* God exists" or "I believe *that* God is almighty," but with "I believe *in God*." To place one's trust in *someone* far surpasses the faith that one attaches to this or that statement coming from or concerning that someone: to trust in God is to show that one believes God *worthy of faith* and that remaining *faithful* is worthwhile.

It is also noteworthy that we do not say "God, I believe in you!" No, we proclaim our faith before the assembly: "I believe in God."

Proclaiming our faith means saying *who* God is and what God has *done* for us. In other words, this act of faith is enriched with meaning.

"I believed, therefore I spoke" (2 Cor 4:13).

Believers cannot be silent about this faith that sustains them. St. Paul could in no way restrain himself from saying "Woe to me if I do not preach [the gospel]!" (1 Cor 9:16).

6

Declaring one's faith in the Lord is everyone's business, each one according to his or her gifts:

"The stumbling block to faith is not that Christ died, but that he rose from the dead. This shocking truth is communicated from neighbor to neighbor, by greater and lesser messengers. It is always contemporary, and each one expresses it in his or her own way, whether as theologian, philosopher, mystic, or artist, or through one's own unique expression of life."

Pierre Emmanuel

Proclaiming the Faith of the Apostles

On the morning of Pentecost, the apostles were the first to proclaim the faith of the Church. This eager proclamation contained three essential points: "Jesus died; God raised him to life; you must repent."

Faith is not meant to be whispered about.

When we celebrate the Eucharist, we echo this proclamation. After the consecration and elevation of the Body and Blood of Christ, we say:

When we eat this bread
and drink this cup,
we proclaim your death, Lord Jesus,
until you come in glory.

Here is the origin of the Creed. This profession of faith in the Father, Son, and Holy Spirit is what we call the Apostles' Creed, sometimes referred to as the "Symbol of the Apostles."

In ancient times, when people wanted to make a pact, their custom was to break an object and distribute its fragments. Each one received a portion of proof that was called a *symbol* (a Greek word meaning "a piece that fits" or "that corresponds to"). It was by putting the pieces together that their correspondence was verified and that people then acknowledged or authenticated their relationship as partners.

What is a "symbol"?

A Christian does not invent his or her own faith. It is received from the Church. One adheres to it by fidelity to the apostles. The Apostles' Creed (Symbol) is the sign of

Receiving the faith from the Church . . .

7

recognition among Christians. It places us in community and unites us with others in the same faith. The "I believe" is first of all a "We believe."

. . . with a converted heart

During the time of preparation for baptism, the candidate, young or adult, receives from the Christian community the words of the Creed and, with it, an initiation into the faith. At the approach to baptism, the candidate is invited to recite or "give" the Creed to the community: with the grace of conversion, he or she solemnly recites the Apostles' Creed before the entire Church and makes the commitment to remain faithful to it.

By this profession of faith converts acknowledge what God "the Father, Son, and Holy Spirit" *does* for them and for all people. They welcome "God's deeds" into their own lives and into the life of the Church and of the world. He or she agrees to put his or her own life in God and to live as a brother or sister.

The Creed—from the Latin *Credo* ("I believe")—has become the main point of reference for a more developed catechesis. During the Liturgy of the Eucharist, we proclaim the Nicene Creed, i.e., the profession of faith that the Church formulated during the Council of Nicaea (325) and endorsed by the Council of Constantinople (381).

In time, our profession of baptismal faith—the Creed— entered the Eucharistic celebration. It appears there as a response to the Word of God. It takes part in the faith dialogue between God and God's people, especially as we recite it during the Sunday celebration.

From baptism to the Eucharist

The Creed conveys its full meaning when it becomes the prayer of the people of God gathered in liturgical assembly, taking on perhaps different shades of meaning at Christmas or at Easter or Pentecost, in time of peace, or in time of persecution! It is the Creed that sets us in communion with all Christians throughout the world.

The Apostles' Creed

I believe in God,
the Father almighty,
creator of heaven and earth.

I believe in Jesus Christ, his only Son, our Lord.
He was conceived by the power of the Holy Spirit,
and born of the Virgin Mary.
He suffered under Pontius Pilate,
was crucified, died, and was buried.
He descended to the dead.
On the third day he rose again.
He ascended into heaven,
and is seated at the right hand of the Father.
He will come again to judge the living and the dead.

I believe in the Holy Spirit,
the holy catholic Church,
the communion of saints,
the forgiveness of sins,
the resurrection of the body,
and life everlasting. Amen.

The Nicene Creed

*We believe in one God,
the Father, the Almighty,
maker of heaven and earth,
of all that is seen and unseen.*

*We believe in one Lord, Jesus Christ,
the only Son of God,
eternally begotten of the Father,
God from God, Light from Light,
true God from true God,
begotten, not made, one in Being with the Father.
Through him all things were made.
For us and for our salvation
he came down from heaven:
by the power of the Holy Spirit
he was born of the Virgin Mary,
and became man.*

*For our sake he was crucified under Pontius Pilate;
he suffered, died, and was buried.
On the third day he rose again
in fulfillment of the Scriptures;
he ascended into heaven
and is seated at the right hand of the Father.
He will come again in glory
to judge the living and the dead,
and his kingdom will have no end.*

*We believe in the Holy Spirit,
the Lord, the giver of life,
who proceeds from the Father and the Son.
With the Father and the Son
he is worshiped and glorified.
He has spoken through the Prophets.*

*We believe in one holy catholic and apostolic Church.
We acknowledge one baptism for the forgiveness of sins.
We look for the resurrection of the dead,
and the life of the world to come. Amen.*

We believe in one God

Christians are not alone in believing in God. Millions of men and women rely on God. Various paths lead us to God, for example, reflection upon nature, upon love, or upon human consciousness. We can prove God's existence by reason, but *faith* in God is a different matter. Other ways also lead to God because they restore in people the image of their Creator. These are the paths of love and devotion. There are many good and upright people who do not share our faith. They are not far from the God in whom we believe. Indeed, believing in God is not limited merely to admitting God's existence, for the believer takes the risk of building an entire life upon God. After such a conversion, life is no longer the same; it acquires a new meaning, takes on a new moral orientation, and is charged with new hope.

Yet who is God for us Christians? God in whom we believe is the Holy Trinity—one God: Father, Son, and Holy Spirit. It is through the Son become man that we have learned to say "Our Father" to God. For us Christians, God speaks and acts in our history: the Christian God is God-with-us.

Before human beings searched for God, God searched for them. The Bible shows God as the one who spoke to the hearts of the first man and woman. God made a covenant with Noah and his companions in the ark, and he chose

In which God do we believe?

11

a people for himself in Abraham, Isaac, Jacob, and the twelve patriarchs; God appeared to Moses in the burning bush and formed a covenant with the Chosen People on Mount Sinai; God spoke through the prophets. God was made man in Jesus, who became "like us in everything except sin," and renewed his covenant by the gift of his life.

"To seek God is to find him" . . .

God is revealed not only in Jesus Christ; God has also given us the Holy Spirit. Through the Spirit we can recognize in Jesus the Son of God. Indeed, ". . . no one can say, 'Jesus is Lord,' except by the holy Spirit" (1 Cor 12:3).

. . . *"to find God is to seek him"*
(St. Augustine).

Nevertheless, God remains beyond all knowledge. By adoring God, we discover him as the one who is love. St. Augustine said, "You are great, Lord, and infinitely worthy of praise. . . . You have made us for yourself, and our hearts are restless until they rest in you." To know God means always to enter further into an attitude of *acknowledging* the Father, the Son, and the holy Spirit.

"This is the will of God, your
holiness" (1 Thess 4:3)

Every day in the Liturgy of the Eucharist we sing "Holy, holy, holy Lord!" This acclamation recalls what Isaiah the prophet heard when he was called (Isa 6:3). We direct it to the Father, the Son, and the Holy Spirit—one God.

God alone is holy. God's holiness shines forth and makes itself known to the angels, the prophets, and the people. The people of God are holy because God has established a relationship with them.

In a world where we are tempted to keep silent about God, Christ invites us to pray to the Father: ". . . hallowed be thy name," i.e., that it be acknowledged by all people (Matt 6:9).

12

The Father almighty

God is the source of all goodness.

Before acknowledging God as "almighty," it is good to discover him as Father. From the first, God is Father in *himself* because within the Holy Trinity, before anything was created, he begets his Son. God is love because love, which is union in the Trinity, has its origin in the Father. Furthermore, he is also *our* Father because he created us and loves us to the point of adopting us as his children.

Do we still have need of a Father?

Every person is deeply marked by the relationship with his or her father and mother: a child does not have it easy in finding a liberating and nourishing context to grow up in. This is true for each of our lives and for all humanity. Hurtful parent-child relationships on the human level can have a bad effect on our relationship with God the Father.

Many false images of God—images we formed perhaps because of a father or a mother who was overprotective or too authoritarian, or of an oppressive or weak-willed father—have aroused anxiety or rebelliousness in individuals. Many of our contemporaries live through this drama: "It's either God or me!" they say. People think that in order to become an adult, they have to eliminate God from their lives, from culture, and from society. On the contrary, could it be that our society is sick *because* of the absence of God? When there is silence about God, many people are left out in the cold by having no father (Father) at all.

The Father gives himself to us.

How could we all be brothers and sisters if we did not have the same Father? If there is *no Father,* there are *no brothers and no sisters.* For the Christian faith, God has always been a God who is lovingly concerned with humans. Jesus says that the Father is good, which means that his presence makes us happy.

God is "Our Father" because in his goodness he has willed his creatures into being. Unfortunately, the image of a severe and repressive God has caused doubt about him. But God loves us so much that he gives us his Son so that we might understand that he wants to be our Father.

"May almighty God bless you, the Father, the Son, and the Holy Spirit." This is the way each Eucharist ends. The one who makes all things exist makes humans exist *for eternity,* for God will never withdraw his life-giving love.

In the same love, Jesus speaks of us as his brothers and sisters, and the Father adopts us as his children when we adopt him as a father. This *mutual adoption* is the key to understanding the covenant between God and human beings.

Often we hear it said, "Why doesn't God do this?" "Why didn't he prevent this catastrophe?" "Does he answer our prayers?" "What is his power?" "How does he use it?"

Can God do everything we imagine?

God has created everything. He has made the universe what it is, and the power of his love manifests itself in everything that exists, and not in everything that we imagine that he could do. It is not "God's fault," then, if people are victims of an earthquake or a hurricane. Despite everything, we know that God remains sovereign in relation to his creatures, and his omnipotence surpasses everything that we could imagine on the subject. The omnipotence of God belongs as well to the mystery of God.

God also intervenes in history and in people's hearts. His omnipotence does not restrict our freedom but rather respects it. We are not his subjects; we are his children.

Creator of heaven and earth, of all that is seen and unseen

Everything that exists, exists through God. From the beginning, creation was like an empty cradle waiting for the birth of humanity. Both hospitable and hostile to humans, the universe offers a place where one can have a good life, but where one must also die. Humanity is called to make the world more humane; such is its calling.

For whom has God made the universe?

Our faith goes even further. Humanity itself has brought this waiting for God into our midst. In a sense, humanity has been the empty cradle waiting for Jesus Christ.

The world is beautiful, its beauty coming primarily from its openness to God toward whom it is directed. The world is not made to turn in upon itself. It is made to be with Christ, since ". . . the Father loves the Son and has given everything over to him" (John 3:35).

Nonetheless, creation has also been entrusted to humans: everything that is has been given to sustain humanity, to make the earth fruitful, and to praise the Creator. All creation has been given to humanity:

All belong[s] to you,
and you to Christ,
and Christ to God (1 Cor 3:22-23).

The Bible tells the story of creation in a poetic manner, with an optimism that cuts through the stories of ancient religions. In the light of its faith in the God of the Covenant, the people of Israel tell us where humanity came from. Throughout its dramatic history, Israel experienced God's fidelity. Day by day, it discovered this unfailing love that was there from the beginning.

How should we understand the Bible stories about the origin of humanity?

The first words of the Bible tell us that in the beginning God created the heavens and the earth. He created everything by his Word. By his breath he gave life to the man he had formed from the soil. The soil is the symbol of our frailty, and breath is the symbol of life. God created male and female in his own image and likeness; for man and woman are the rulers of the whole universe to the extent that they are the image of God, i.e., ruling the world with intelligence and love.

Do these stories conflict with science?

Has God created the world "once and for all"?

What is the world headed toward?

The Bible and science offer two viewpoints on the world and humanity. While the Bible is concerned with the "why" of things, science asks questions about the "how." They are two different viewpoints, yet they are complementary, even convergent. The Bible reveals to humanity the meaning of its existence and directs us toward a life of faith.

The colorful stories in the Bible that tell us how God creates, protects, and rules the universe express a deep reality. They speak in symbolic language. The Genesis story of creation (Gen 1–11) is in some way "truer" than any of our learned accounts and reconstructions about the past. It is a faith-informed recounting of how human beings experience their liberty and its limits, the presence of evil and their own free contribution to it, and of their experience of God's power and goodness.

The whole universe comes from God. It comes today just as it came at the first instant. The world has its own stability, but it does not exist by itself; it exists by the will of God, who never stops creating and sustaining life. Our dependence on God does not make us slaves to him. The person who recognizes the goodness of the Creator knows that life and the world are given to him or her each day, as a gift.

God does not keep the universe in existence as if he were acting from a distance. He leads men and women and all creation toward his Son, who was given for us. Far from being absurd, it is for this reason that the world, guided by Providence, flows toward its complete fulfillment. When God acts as our guide, there is no negation of human freedom. On the contrary!

18

To say that God is Providence does not mean that everything has been arranged in advance or that he acts in place of us. In everything, and in all that happens to us as human beings, God desires our well-being. There is a profound optimism in this that argues against every kind of determinism or fatalism.

"We have to believe in Providence!" people still say (but how little!).

People do not create, but they *collaborate* with God's creation. They discover the hidden riches of creation, and continually find new, latent possibilities in the universe that God has entrusted to them. Human beings possess an extraordinary capacity for invention: every day they can produce new things in all kinds of areas (art, technology, language, etc.). In this they are the image of their Creator. But can humans allow themselves to do everything they are capable of? Such a question introduces the idea of morality. The inventiveness of human beings ought to be filled with the law of love that they receive from God.

Are humans also creators?

Every day newspapers, radio, and television tell us about terrible happenings, many of which are caused by human action. Sin weighs heavily upon the world, and evil dwells in our hearts. It wounds us deep down in our most intimate selves and corrupts our relations with God, with others, and with ourselves.

Are not humanity and the world completely disoriented?

Men and women accept the human condition with difficulty. If we cannot accept ourselves as creatures, then we cannot accept God. We are weak beings whose bodies are vulnerable to sickness, accident, and death. Some of us die without having really lived. Humans count for little when nature is unleashed. But despite everything, we love life with all its pleasures and joys.

What is "original sin"?

In each of us a voice prompts us to rebel against God: Why were we made so fragile and vulnerable? The Bible speaks to us about this rebelliousness (Gen 3). From the beginning, says the Bible, people dreamed of being God and of knowing everything, both good and evil. To live at the center of our being, to be rulers of our fate, to know everything, and to live without dying—this is the dream that lives in us. But it is not reality. Faced with petty thoughts, humans become fearful and alarmed. The universe was created for human beings to find their way to God. But humanity has failed in this task by making itself, not God, the focus of attention. This is indeed why the world is so disoriented.

Adam, Eve, and the serpent: what do they mean? (Gen 2:4–3:24).

Genesis speaks about original sin. It portrays the first man and woman in ways that every human being can identify with. The Garden of Eden represents the primal happiness that God gave humankind. Everything was given to them. They could eat fruit from all the trees in the garden except one: the tree of the knowledge of good and evil. That fruit was reserved for God himself and was forbidden. But even though Adam and Eve had not created themselves or their consciences, even though they had not determined what was good and what was evil, nevertheless, they wanted to be like their Creator. They wanted to taste the forbidden fruit that God had placed off-limits to them. And so they acted against God and chose to conduct their lives without him.

The Expulsion. Joseph O'Connell.
Engraving. 15" x 10."

20

When we sin, we spontaneously try to excuse ourselves by casting blame on someone else or on other causes outside of ourselves. "It was not I," says Adam, "It was Eve!" Eve blames the serpent, the sly one. When we are in the grip of sin, the evil comes from within us, but it takes us by surprise, as if coming from outside: we are seduced by it. The fate of the first couple is that of all humanity. Indeed, we experience our weakness every day, and it is truly by our free choice that we transgress the law of God. However, the story in Genesis also says that the man and woman did not initiate the revolt against God: they sinned, but only after they had first been seduced. This corresponds to our own experience. When we come into the world, evil is already there. We submit to it and become its accomplices.

We are not evil by nature, even in the depth of our being; on the contrary, says the Bible, humankind has been created good, and it is by falling for the tricks of the Evil One that we become sinners. Thus, as victims and accomplices of evil, we all need to be saved.

Jesus—the new Adam

In the Christian view, Jesus is given to us as the "new Adam" through whom sin and death are conquered. Eve is the mother of the living; Mary is the Mother of Jesus and of the faithful. She is the "new Eve," the mother of a new humanity.

Original sin is the latent complicity with evil of every person, from the first instance of our existence. Through baptism, the Christian is reborn to a new life in Christ, freed from original sin because in us dwells the Spirit of God, whose very love sustains our being.

It is difficult to believe that creation is limited to visible beings. In the Old Testament, angels make up part of God's invisible entourage, and they act as intermediaries between God and human beings. In the New Testament, they intervene at decisive moments in salvation history: at the annunciation, the nativity, at the times when Jesus was tempted in the desert and at Gethsemane, the resurrection, and the ascension. They manifest who Jesus is. They will come with the Lord when he comes again in glory. Even today, the liturgy celebrates guardian angels, St. Michael, St. Gabriel, St. Raphael, and all the angels.

What about angels?

Of course, Christians are admonished not to neglect their earthly tasks. But that doesn't mean that they should automatically deny what is invisible. God's creation is infinitely

Are these beliefs of the past?

21

greater than we suspect. Can we reduce angels to figments of the imagination simply because they do not fit into our rationalist mentality?

In the light of Scripture, the Church believes that angels exist, that they are creatures of God, immortal beings, endowed with knowledge and freedom. Servants of God, they share in the work of salvation. It is true that we have to get beyond the imagery! However, the action of angels in the service of Christ continues even today. Every day in celebrating the Eucharist the Church joins in praising them when it sings "Holy, holy, holy Lord . . . heaven and earth are filled with your glory!" Angels are close to God and close to human beings.

Does Satan exist? Demons or evil forces play a role in most religions. They play an even greater role in certain magical practices, in groups that seek to hallucinate, and in sects that claim to be in the service of Satan. Today sorcery thrives even in the most technological civilizations. It continues to traffic in fear. Worse, it makes people believe that the world is created and ruled by Satan.

What is Satan's power? *Satan,* in Hebrew, means "opponent." In Greek, he is called the "devil," "he who divides," and "he who accuses." Jesus begins his public life in the desert where he is led by the Holy Spirit; Satan tempts Jesus; he goes so far as to say to him, "Worship me. . . ." But Jesus unmasks and defeats him. Satan tempts the disciples, he enters into Judas, he tests all men and women individually and collectively; ultimately, he will be conquered at the last judgment.

God has created human beings *free,* that is, with an innate ability to do good. And if this freedom suffers because of our sins and by the sins of our associates, Christ restores it.

The Church invites us to stand up to the devil (1 Pet 5:9), to resist everything that comes from deceit, trickery, and lies, for Satan tries to manipulate the human heart and shackle our freedom. The Church invites us to be watchful and to pray lest we fall into temptation. In its teaching, it speaks of the mystery of evil just as much as it speaks of its belief in Christ, the conqueror of evil. It is in union with the Risen Christ that the baptized experience the power of sharing in the victory of Christ over evil in one's self and in the world.

The Christian spirit is resolutely optimistic; in the Lord, nei-

22

ther evil nor death will have the last word. Fatalism is not a Christian attitude.

We believe in one Lord, Jesus Christ, the only Son of God . . .

Nowadays, Christians of all persuasions are displaying a renewed interest in Jesus Christ. Beginning with their personal experience and their various commitments, they ask themselves, "Who is he, really? What is his role in history?" This interest is not limited to the Christian world. Jews, Muslims, atheists, and agnostics turn as well with curiosity or interest toward the person of Jesus.

A current question: Who is Jesus Christ?

We are so used to hearing the expression "Jesus Christ" that we do not always realize that each of these titles—Christ, Son, Lord—designates Jesus at successive levels of understanding and faith. How did this faith develop in the time of the disciples and the first Christians?

A question on several levels

Jesus is a common name in Israel. It means "God saves." Born to a humble Jewish family, Jesus lived in Nazareth, a small village in Galilee. The running joke there was to ask if anything good could come from Nazareth.

"Jesus," an ordinary name

Upon seeing the man and hearing his exceptional witness, his contemporaries sided either for or against him. Many admired him; some followed him. They recognized Jesus as the one who not only proclaimed the Kingdom and healed the sick but also pardoned sins. Now God alone can forgive sins. Who then is this man? The disciples witnessed Jesus' behavior in relation to the Law and the Temple. They discovered his particular relation to God, whom he called by a familiar name: *Abba,* that is, "Father," or closer to our vernacular "Daddy."

Who is this man who has the power to forgive sins?

Jesus did not just announce the coming of the Kingdom; he also led people to understand that the Kingdom of God *is here.* Although he did not say explicitly that he was God, his witness and his behavior gave indications of the "mystery" of his person. The disciples were thus led to ask themselves even more searchingly about his identity: "Who then is this whom even wind and sea obey?" (Mark 4:41).

With Jesus' death and resurrection and continuing through the experience of the Easter appearances, the disciples, at first distressed by their master's execution, gradually discovered that he was alive: God had raised him up from the dead. In him life triumphed over death. In the light of this experience and the Old Testament prophecies, they began to remember everything that Jesus had shared with them from the beginning of his public life. It was then, by the gift of the Spirit on Pentecost, that the apostles perceived that God had manifested himself in Jesus with all of his saving power. "In the name of Jesus" they preached and worked miracles; they baptized and forgave sins.

"Of Mary was born Jesus who is called Christ" (Matt 1:16, JB).

Christ is a Greek word that means "the anointed one"; it corresponds to the Hebrew term *Messiah*. In giving this title to Jesus, the disciples recognized that in him the Scriptures were fulfilled: he was the Anointed of God. It was God the Father, and not human beings, who consecrated him as Savior by pouring out his Spirit upon him.

Jesus is the Christ; we do not expect any other or recognize any other, even if people chant, "Messiahs! Messiahs! Every man and woman is a messiah, and there are over five billion of us!" Only one can save us: Jesus Christ. This is our faith.

Is a Christian another Christ?

Through baptism and confirmation, every Christian has been anointed and shares in the very life of Christ. Since the earliest times of the Church, the baptized are called "christs": they are anointed with the "perfume of gladness" to carry the Good News to those without hope. It is God who consecrates them and sends them forth.

When we communicate with the Body and Blood of Christ, we become one body with him. "And so," it was said to the newly baptized, "we become 'Christ-bearers' with his Body and his Blood shared among us members."

"There is one Lord, Jesus Christ" (1 Cor 8:6, JB).

A lord has everything at his disposal. Israel called its God Yahweh (lord) because he had created his people and everything else. Yahweh was the Lord of the universe and of all peoples. Compared with political powers and idols, Yahweh was the *only* Lord.

The early Christians called the Risen Jesus "the Lord": they recognized in him the same sovereignty that God has. Jesus is the source of life. By dying he gave us his divine life. He has cast "his enemies at his feet"—evil, suffering, and death.

We proclaim that Jesus is "the only Lord," the only one with the right to claim our obedience in faith, since he be-

24

came the Servant of all. "Because of this, God greatly exalted him . . . so that . . . every tongue confesses that Jesus
Christ is Lord" (Phil 2:9-11).

In proclaiming that Jesus is Lord, we affirm his divinity. God
has manifested himself in Christ's humanity. Jesus Christ
presents himself as "the Son," for God is his Father in a
special way and shares with him everything that belongs
to him. In revealing his Father, Jesus revealed his identity
as Son (John 5:19-30). God has but one Son, which means
that he has given him all his love. He possesses the divine
nature of the Father and the Holy Spirit; "God from God
. . . true God from true God, begotten, not made, one in
Being with the Father" (Nicene Creed). From the moment
of baptism we are "adopted" children of God, since we
share in his divine nature.

"The only Son of God."

Light is a symbol of happiness, joy, and life. It comes from
God: Jesus is "Light from Light." God is neither a threat
nor a "wet blanket" for us. On the contrary, he gives life.
Jesus is the true light; he wages combat against the darkness, and every baptized person is called upon to reject the
works of darkness in order to live in light, truth, and justice.

"Light from light"

25

By the power of the Holy Spirit, he was born of the Virgin Mary and became man

Why wasn't Jesus conceived like other human beings?

Jesus is a gift of God, an incomparable gift. Conceived by the Holy Spirit, he was born of the Virgin Mary. This is the core of the Good News expressed in the first pages of the Gospels of Matthew and Luke. It is on this basis that the Church professes Mary's virginity: the fact that she gave birth to Jesus although she had not known man (Luke 1:34).

There is more here than the fact that "nothing [is] impossible for God" (Luke 1:37). Above all, the virginal conception declares *who* is the promised child. It brings us into the heart of the mystery of the person of Christ.

"He took flesh of the Virgin Mary": why this expression?

In Jesus, God has taken our flesh. The Hebrew word for "flesh" designates the entire person considered in his or her frailty. Formed in his mother's womb, Jesus was born "in the flesh." Mary and Joseph loved their little one as he cried. In him, God took on the eyes of a baby, and with his tiny feet he had to learn to walk in human steps. He

learned to talk from Mary, and from Joseph he learned his trade. "Christ passed through each human age and therefore provides for everyone communion with God" (St. Irenaeus). He knew hunger, temptation, suffering, and abandonment. He was like us in everything but sin.

The Gospels present Mary as the mother of the Son of God. Jesus' entire childhood unfolded in his mother's shadow. When God spoke to her, he awaited the "yes" that was spoken for the entire human race. Yet if Mary could say "yes," it was only by God's grace; this response has its source in the "yes" of Christ to his Father. That is why the prayer of the entire Church makes Mary's answer its own: "May it be done to me according to your word."

Mary's "yes"

Mary's unreserved obedience was not possible without the love that came from God. Her heart was free from original sin, entirely untouched by it; she was without any thought for herself. For Mary had been saved by him who died for her, he to whom she gave life. From eternity God had chosen Mary to be the mother of his Son, which is why she was "full of grace": the Love of God had enveloped her since her own conception and had preserved her free from all sin. This is the mystery that we joyfully celebrate on December 8, the feast of the Immaculate Conception.

Why was Mary preserved from original sin?

When we speak of Mary's purity—of her Immaculate Conception—we are not speaking, as many think, of the procreative act by which Mary was begotten by her parents, nor are we speaking of the virginal conception of Jesus. We are speaking, rather, of the absence of original sin from the first moment of her existence, of the purity of her unfailing orientation toward God. This grace is the Father's gift to Mary.

Detail from Group of Founding Nuns. Joseph O'Connell. Stone. 36" high. Gathering Place, St. Benedict's Convent, St. Joseph, Minnesota.

Hail Mary

Hail Mary,
full of grace,
the Lord is with thee.
Blessed art thou among women
and blessed is the fruit of thy womb, Jesus.
Holy Mary, Mother of God,
pray for us sinners
now and at the hour of our death.
Amen.

Mary owes everything to grace. That is why the Church sings in the "Magnificat" about the marvels that the Lord has done for Mary. The Church recognizes its calling in her who was the first to believe in Jesus and to accept him from God. She recognizes in Mary the "new Eve," the first of the faithful to seize upon the fruit of redemption.

Song of Mary (Magnificat)

My soul proclaims the greatness of the Lord;
my spirit rejoices in God my Savior.
For he has looked upon his handmaid's lowliness;
behold, from now on will all ages call me blessed.
The Mighty One has done great things for me,
and holy is his Name.
His mercy is from age to age to those who fear him.
He has shown might with his arm,
dispersed the arrogant of mind and heart.
He has thrown down the rulers from their thrones
but lifted up the lowly.
The hungry he has filled with good things;
the rich he has sent away empty.
He has helped Israel his servant,
remembering his mercy,
according to his promise to our fathers,
to Abraham and to his descendants forever.

That Mary is the mother of Jesus of Nazareth is easily understood. But that a woman should be the mother of God is certainly beyond understanding! For the first Christians, Jesus was not a man who became a son of God, but was the Son of God who became man. Thus Christ is fully God and fully man, two distinct natures in one being. Mary is his mother: mother of God and mother of Jesus the man. We celebrate this mystery eight days after Christmas, the first day of the year, as the feast of Mary, Mother of God.

Mary and the Church resemble each other. Just as in Mary virginity and motherhood are indissolubly united, so they are in the Church as well. Mary conceives the Father's Son by her faith and by the Holy Spirit. The Church gives birth to the divine life of the Father's adopted children by the purity of its message and by baptism.

28

Mary is our mother because Christ, from the cross, gave her to his disciple John, and through him to all the disciples: "Woman, behold, your son."—"[Son], behold your mother" (John 19:27).

The whole people of God turn toward Mary.

Devotion to Mary should be rid of clichés that make her a woman between heaven and earth or a humble, passive, submissive girl, a model for an unattractive religiosity. On the contrary, Mary reflects the hopes and aspirations of the men and women of our time. And her virginity is not a negation of the values of marriage; her "yes" is a courageous choice.

As a woman in whom the Holy Spirit dwells, the Virgin is not afraid to proclaim that God lifts up the lowly and the oppressed and casts down the mighty from their thrones. She holds first place among the poor: she was a strong woman who experienced poverty, suffering, flight, and exile. Christians who in their evangelical spirit want to harness the forces of freedom to the service of humanity and society, turn to Mary. For in her motherhood, Mary is not confined to her only son. At the foot of the cross her love takes on a universal dimension.

Throughout the world the angelic salutation is raised: "Hail Mary, full of grace." The Angelus, the pilgrimages, rosaries, and millions of lighted candles declare the unanimous praise of the people. As icons portray, Mary shows us *Christ;* she shows us the Way.

The Angelus

The Angel of the Lord made the announcement to Mary,
and she conceived by the Holy Spirit.

> HAIL MARY . . .

Behold the handmaid of the Lord;
let it be done to me according to your Word.

> HAIL MARY . . .

And the Word was made flesh,
and dwelt among us.

> HAIL MARY . . .

Pray for us, holy Mother of God,
that we may be made worthy of the promises of Christ.
Let us pray.
Pour out your grace upon our hearts, O Lord, that we
to whom the incarnation of your Son, Jesus Christ, was
made known by the message of an angel, by his passion
and cross may come to the glory of his resurrection.
Through the same Christ, our Lord.
Amen.

The Rosary

The Joyful Mysteries

Annunciation to Mary
Visitation of Mary to Elizabeth
Nativity of Jesus in Bethlehem
Presentation of Jesus in the temple
Finding of Jesus in the temple

The Sorrowful Mysteries

Agony of Jesus in the Garden of Olives
Scourging of Jesus
Crowning with thorns
Carrying of the cross
Crucifixion and death of Jesus

The Glorious Mysteries

Resurrection of Jesus
Ascension of Jesus into heaven
Sending of the Holy Spirit
Assumption of the Virgin Mary
Coronation of Mary in heaven

He was crucified under Pontius Pilate, he suffered, died, and was buried.

Jesus' entire life was the source of salvation, since everything he said and did was pleasing to God. In the Creed, his earthly existence is summed up in his passion and crucifixion. The Church teaches us that Jesus' death is not merely the consequence of his prophetic commitment. The Lord's death and resurrection are the basis for our salvation. By enduring his extreme humiliation Jesus proved his limitless love for humankind and his unfailing obedience to the Father who sent him. "Because of this, God greatly exalted him . . . [so] that at the name of Jesus every knee should bend. . . ." (Phil 2:9-10).

The death of Jesus is often seen as a drama in itself. One pictures God sending his Son to death, and attention is drawn to the horror of the crucifixion more than to the love that Jesus exhibited. But it is not the death of Jesus that saves us; it is his unconditional *love* made manifest by his death.

"He came to what was his own, but his own people did not accept him" (John 1:11). This drama reveals the tragic dimension of all human history: God's love has been rejected by human beings.

The Father allowed his Son, truly human among humans, to suffer the same lot his brothers and sisters are exposed to in a world indifferent to love.

All the Father's love is present in his Son, his well-beloved, who suffers. In Jesus, God appears to us as one who never abandons humanity and who goes with us to the limit of our pain and distress.

Every day, suffering and death are fearful realities for thousands of men and women. Many die for just causes and for human rights. Why then is such importance attached to Jesus' death? It is because his death is not merely that of a just man humiliated and sacrificed. If Jesus were not God, his death would be just another death.

One who loves suffers even worse by virtue of his love. And no one loves us as much as God loves us!

Was the crucifixion the only way to save us?

Why didn't the Father prevent his Son's death?

How many human beings have suffered more than Jesus?

31

Who will help us glimpse the hidden meaning of the cross?

By disregarding the fact that God reveals himself to us on the cross, we risk reducing Christianity to a general humanism. A man wanted to build a better world and died from his efforts. That's not about salvation, but about defeat! Only the Spirit of the Father could make the apostles understand the meaning of Jesus' death on the cross. It was on Pentecost that they received that revelation.

How is the death of Jesus unique?

The Gospels describe for us Jesus' death as a manifestation of God in his Son. In the light of the Scriptures, St. Matthew writes that at the moment when Jesus died, the "tombs were opened, and the bodies of many saints who had fallen asleep were raised" (Matt 27:52-53). This sentence has a meaning for our faith. It tells us that he who died on the cross is not only a man; he is Lord of the living and the dead! In him, God manifests himself. Through him, death is conquered and life triumphs. St. John describes Jesus on the cross as one who "handed over the Spirit" (John 19:30). The expression is very strong. The Spirit of God is given to us as the Son expires. The death of Christ is unique because the Son of God is unique.

Why is the cross of Christ a font of salvation?

Everything Jesus said and did is found to be sealed on the cross. Jesus' death is not understood if it is cut off from his life: "I came so that they might have life and have it more abundantly" (John 10:10). This life is God's own life. It is not a life that is ended by death, but a life that crosses through death. Jesus did not recoil in the face of death; he confronted it in the name of life. He *is* the Life.

"No one takes [my life] from me.
But I lay it down on my own.
I have power to lay it down,
and power to take it up again."

So says Jesus in the parable of the Good Shepherd (John 10:18). Surely many shepherds, in the image of their master, have given their lives for their flocks. Yet who among them ever had the power to take up their lives again? Who is the master of life? Contemplating the mystery of Jesus' death on the cross, John sees water and blood gush from the open wound in Christ's side. Water is the source of life: it indicates baptism. Blood is life: it indicates the Eucharist.

What is the meaning of Jesus "redeeming" us by his death?

The richness of the mystery of God revealed in Jesus Christ is such that the first Christians did not have the wherewithal to speak of it. Along with the apostles, they stammered. The

New Testament writings speak of "ransom" and "redemption," of the sacrifice and offering of Christ to his Father. These are very expressive words for someone who knows what it means to free a slave or pay to obtain his freedom. Christ pays *with his person:* he buys our freedom with love, a love that nothing stops—neither death nor contempt.

". . . only with difficulty does one die for a just person. . . . [Yet] while we were still sinners, Christ died for us!" (Rom 5:7-8).

Why do Christians pray, "Lamb of God, you take away the sins of the world . . ." before communicating with the Body and Blood of Christ dead and risen?

Is Jesus' death a sacrifice?

Jesus' crucifixion appeared to the early Christians as the fulfillment of the offering of the Paschal lamb (John 19:36). The disciples lived through the heartrending moment of Christ's death on the outskirts of Jerusalem at the time when lambs were being slaughtered in the temple court for the celebration of Passover. For us Christians, Christ is the Paschal Lamb above all others.

The prophecy of Isaiah was also fulfilled by Jesus' passion: "Like a lamb led to the slaughter . . . he was silent and opened not his mouth" (Isa 53:7). In this canticle the "Suffering Servant" takes away the people's sins and leads the faithless and scattered flocks back to unity.

The early Christian communities, challenged by persecution, sang canticles to the Lamb, slain but victorious, wounded but alive (Rev 4–5)! The Church repeats these canticles every week in evening prayer.

The cross is so commonplace that we can see it as a mere ornament and not be troubled by it! Nonetheless, it reveals to us the depth of human sin, the ability to answer love with hate. The cross shows us the face of God with his pierced heart, the wellspring of mercy. It tells us that every disciple who wants to follow Christ will inevitably run into indifference and contempt; but in Christ, the cross represents victory all the same. The cross does not teach submission, and suffering is not sacred. It is either to be struggled against or borne with love. For it is love that the cross brings about.

Do you have a crucifix? Then look at the Crucified and believe!

The cross is not the last word. Yet without it, there is no

victory over death for those who want to overcome the strife within themselves and in the world.

The cross is the sign of the Christian: one makes the sign of the cross to enter—body and soul—into an attitude of love for God and self-giving toward other people. Parents teach their children the sign of the cross and like to trace it on their foreheads.

He rose from the dead, ascended into heaven, and sits at the right hand of the Father

The cup of faith!

All those implicated in Jesus' death were overtaken by the events leading to it and reacted badly: Caiphas, Pilate, Judas, Peter . . . The apostles were timid and cowardly at the time of the crucifixion. In contrast, they fearlessly testified to the Lord's resurrection: "God has made him both Lord and Messiah, this Jesus whom you crucified!" cried Peter on Pentecost (Acts 2:36).

What is Christ's resurrection?

The resurrection of Christ is actual fact. Yet there are two things to consider about it. First of all, the resurrection has a noticeable historical dimension. It left an indelible mark on human history: the empty tomb, the appearances, the apostles' proclamation of faith at victory over death, and the birth of the Church. Secondly, the resurrection is the very act, impossible for us, by which God brings Jesus of

Nazareth into his glory. He raises him from the dead. This is what we express by proclaiming that Jesus "is seated at the right hand of the Father" and that "God made him Lord."

This paschal mystery, through which Jesus "passes over" from this world to the Father's glory, begins at the hour of Jesus' death: "Father . . . give glory to your Son!" (John 17:1).

God does not act as a miracle worker for human beings in order to dazzle us. He does everything with wisdom and love. Jesus died out of love for us. This is why God raised him from the dead, exalted him, and gave him the glory that is rightly his as Son. "God raised the Lord and will also raise us by his power" (1 Cor 6:14).

Why did God raise him from the dead?

God's act of raising his Son from the dead defies our understanding, and none of the Gospels describe it. The four Gospels do speak about the discovery of the empty tomb. Mary Magdalene cries, "They have taken the Lord from the tomb, and we don't know where they put him" (John 20:2). The empty tomb is the telling sign that reflects the mystery. This indirect sign delivers its full meaning in light of the angels' message: "Why do you seek the living one among the dead?" (Luke 24:5).

What is the apostles' faith in the resurrection based on?

The appearances attest considerably to the presence of the Risen One. Jesus is no longer simply someone that somebody sees because he has arrived at a particular place, or someone that nobody sees because he has gone to another place. As the Risen One, he *makes himself seen:* he "appears" and disappears at Jerusalem or in Galilee, in the Upper Room or on the road to Emmaus, because he is always with us, even when no one sees him.

What do the appearances mean?

The Risen One's presence escapes our present-day human vision, but Jesus visibly manifested himself to the early witnesses. The narratives that come down to us recount two kinds of appearances: those to certain people (the women, Mary Magdalene, the disciples at Emmaus) and those to the apostles, from the evening of Easter up until the ascension, both in Jerusalem and in Galilee.

The last narratives contain a mission mandate for the apostles: "Go, therefore, and make disciples of all nations (Matt 28:19); "As the Father has sent me, so I send you" (John 20:21).

The appearances: an experience of the Church

Paul and Luke mention an appearance to Peter alone (1 Cor 15:5; Luke 24:34). In this testimony the Easter faith of Peter precedes that of the Eleven; faith in the Risen One is the foundation of the Church. In the other narratives it is along with Peter that the Eleven go through the experience of incredulity, then of recognition, and then of the mission mandate.

These appearance narratives tell how the Church is born of the Spirit, the source of faith in the Risen One, and how it rests upon the apostles' collegial faith.

Was Jesus' resurrection just wishful thinking on the part of the apostles? The Gospels present it to us as an event which caught the apostles by surprise and which imposed itself despite their incredulity. Thus when the women brought them the news of the resurrection, they thought that they were talking nonsense and did not believe them (Luke 24:11). When Jesus himself appeared to them, they could not believe it and remained stupefied (Luke 24:37-41). Thomas did not believe what the others told him until Christ appeared to him as well. Paul encountered the Risen One on the road to Damascus, and this experience irresistibly overcame him despite the delight he took in his furious persecution of believers.

Was Jesus' resurrection the product of the apostles' imagination?

By his death and resurrection Jesus saves all humanity. Eastern Christians often represent Christ's death and resurrection by the descent into hell, the abode of the dead. Christ went down to it burdened with human sins; his stigmata were proof of that. He went to seek the dead of all the ages, those who lay in the darkness and in the shadow of death: Adam, Eve, the patriarchs, rulers, the pagans. At their center Christ, radiant with light, appears as Master of life. Hands reach out to him. His hand lifts us out of death. The forced doors and broken locks are evidence of the Spirit's dynamic power against the doors and bolts that keep us prisoners of death.

What is meant by "he descended into hell"?

Jesus' descent into hell emphasizes the fact that he was truly dead. His ascent into heaven, where he is "seated at the right hand of God" signifies that he is "Lord": having conquered death, he reigns with the Father.

"He descended into hell and ascended into heaven."

"His kingdom will have no end," we proclaim in the Creed. This expression indicates that Christ reigns not only in space but also throughout all time. For our daily lives this means that all things, including our past and our future plans, find their meaning in the Risen One. Therefore our lives are completely under the Lord's care every day.

Does Christ's resurrection change history and human life?

Christ rose from the dead at a specific moment in history. In some way, however, he is waiting to "rise again" in the history of a multitude of human lives, a "resurrection" that presupposes everyone's collaboration.

God is not resigned to human death. Nor does he want us to be resigned to it any longer. On the contrary, he calls us to participate in being delivered from deadly selfishness.

Humanity would resign itself to death if it aspired to nothing higher than earthly realities. Earth left to itself does not possess the leaven of immortality.

In Jesus dead and risen, men and women are invited to share, with courage and responsibility, in the action of the God of the living.

Where people lovingly share with others in need, there Christ is today—in a sense, risen from the dead. Where faith leads to an effective commitment to justice and inspires a true desire for peace, there death withdraws and Christ's life is affirmed. Where someone dies who has lived in faith and love and has offered up of his or her sufferings, there the resurrection of Christ brings the hope of new life.

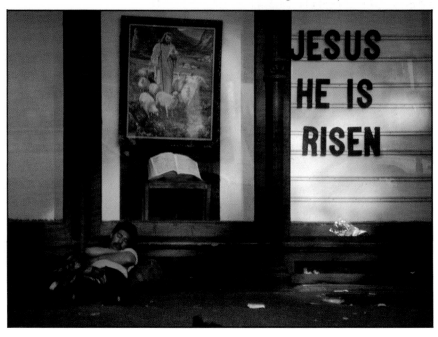

38

He will come again in glory to judge the living and the dead

The profession of faith of the first Christians was directed toward the Lord's return: "Come, Lord Jesus." This final cry of the New Testament is the impatient answer to the Lord's promise: "Yes, I am coming soon!" (Rev 22:20). Are we so attached to the values of the present world that we have lost this impatience and doubt the need to await the Lord's return?

Do we still await the return of Christ?

Every night, thousands of nuns and monks rise before daybreak to chant the Vigils. Through their vocation their whole being awaits the Lord's return. They await on behalf of the Church and the world. They stand watch to wake humanity from its sleep so that it might be able to go out joyfully to meet the Lord. They await the sun who "will visit us" (Luke 1:78) every day in every circumstance, in human relations and in the sacraments. Did he not say, "I am with you always, until the end of the age" (Matt 28:20)?

"Therefore, let us not sleep as the rest do, but let us stay alert and sober!" (1 Thess 5:6).

39

Waiting persistently!

Every year during Advent (which means "coming"), the Church prepares fervently for the coming of Christ in celebrating the mystery of Christmas. The feast of Christmas is not only a remembrance of Jesus' birth; it also celebrates his presence in our day and announces his definitive coming at the end of time. If our faith makes us aware of many advents, they all depend upon the parousia, the final coming of the Lord for the universal judgment. This is why we sing "Christ *has come,* Christ *will come again,* Christ *is here,*" and why we keep watch over our faith.

How can we understand God's judgment?

When the Scriptures state that God judges the world, they proclaim that he is "King," that he governs the universe and orients history toward the salvation of all men and women. The judgment of God is comparable to what people judge to be either meritorious or empty. It is often compared to a purifying fire. To judge is not simply to determine what is good and what is bad; it is also to enhance what is better, like the fire that draws off dross.

Will we be judged?

To say that God is master of history and that Christ is Lord is to affirm the primacy of the universal judgment, linked to the end of time, at the last coming of Christ. The particular judgment of each one of us takes place throughout our lives, at our important choices, and also at the hour of our death. The particular judgment is not fully understood outside the context of a universal judgment at the end of time.

"Rejoice in the Lord always . . . The Lord is near" (Phil 4:4–5).

The presence of God builds us up day by day: ". . . although our outer self is wasting away, our inner self is being renewed day by day" (2 Cor 4:16). Nothing we experience or suffer for the Lord is in vain! In every situation, even the most trying, the power of hope will prevail over the powers of evil, which do not come from God. The attitude to have, then, toward the judgment of God, the font of salvation, is not fear but trust.

Scripture, however, does not conceal from us that there is also a judgment of condemnation, and that the end of time will also be a day of wrath for anyone who stubbornly refuses God's salvation. Evil will be condemned and good rewarded. We should be afraid lest our faith be dormant, lest our conversion not be sincere, lest our love be cooled, and our life built upon sand rather than rock. We hope and ask for God's grace so that day by day he will change our hearts of stone into human hearts capable of receiving him with joy, impatient for his coming and for his saving judgment.

40

The Church has suffered violence and persecution from apostolic times to now. And skeptics ask that if all this is in vain, is it worth the trouble to confront mockery or death in the name of the faith?

To his disciples Jesus said, "And do not be afraid of those who kill the body but cannot kill the soul; rather, be afraid of the one who can destroy both body and soul in Gehenna. . . . So do not be afraid." He adds, "Everyone who acknowledges me before others I will acknowledge before my heavenly Father. But whoever denies me before others, I will deny before my heavenly Father" (Matt 10:28, 31, 32-33).

Do we have reason to believe?

Not all witnesses suffer the extreme of bloodshed. Not everyone is, in the strict sense, a witness (in Greek, *martyr*) of the faith. Yet Jesus said to everyone, "If anyone wishes to come after me, he must deny himself and take up his cross daily and follow me. . . . Whoever is ashamed of me and of my words, the Son of Man will be ashamed of when he comes in his glory and in the glory of the Father and of the holy angels" (Luke 9:23, 26).

Does our faith stand the test?

From today onward, our attachment to Christ gives us inspiration and courage. In building our life on the faith, we build it upon rock. The Risen One whom we welcome into our lives dwells with the Father; where he is, there we shall also be. In accepting our brothers and sisters and in giving up our goods, we receive God along with all those who have built their lives on the faith. The Church will not be "God's assembly" completely until the end of time.

"For whoever wishes to save his life will lose it, but whoever loses his life for my sake will save it" (Luke 9:24).

Christians will be judged upon their faith in Christ, their hope against the whole world, and their love that builds the Church and cares for the poor and the suffering.

On what will we be judged?

God does not judge as human beings do; he does not primarily consider our deeds, but rather he considers the love that we have given. To all those who will have lived in God's love, Jesus will say, "Come, you who are blessed by my Father. Inherit the kingdom prepared for you from the foundation of the world. For I was hungry and you gave me food, I was thirsty and you gave me drink, a stranger and you welcomed me, naked and you clothed me, ill and you cared for me, in prison and you visited me." Then we will all ask, "Lord, when did we see you hungry and feed you, or thirsty and give you drink? When did we see you a stranger and welcome you, or naked and clothe you?

41

When did we see you ill or in prison?" And he will answer, "Whatever you did for one of these least brothers of mine, you did for me" (Matt 25:34-40). For us men and women of the twentieth century this call is directed not only toward personal conversion but also toward the transformation of the structures of our society.

We will be judged by our love. Yet we can still harden our hearts. The Lord warns us, ". . . what you did not do for one of these least ones, you did not do for me" (Matt 25:45). This judgment is a condemnation. The Scriptures show us how God is personally offended when his love is scorned.

Does God judge us, or do we judge ourselves?

The last judgment belongs to God. He gives to whom he pleases, and his mercy will surpass all our merits. His love searches us out even in the shadows, yet he can also judge us for our contempt.

What seems more terrible to us: that God judges us? that others judge us? that our conscience judges us? At times when our conscience allows no appeal, the grace and

mercy of God go before us. Even when we are clearly tempted to despair, God lifts us up through hope. This is how we shall know . . . and reassure our hearts before him in whatever our hearts condemn, for God is greater than our hearts and knows everything (1 John 3:19-20).

The time of the coming of the Son of Man remains the Father's secret. His coming is as certain as the dawn, but his hour is unknown. Even Jesus stated that he did not know it (Mark 13:32). The Gospel says nothing about it; the precise moment is not the concern of Jesus or of human beings. It is the Father's secret.

Therefore, it is not really Christian to want to determine when this event will take place. The Christian has only one attitude appropriate for awaiting the day of the Lord: to be always *ready*. Indeed, the time is always running out for doing good. To do good without interruption is the urgency, and it cannot be put off on the grounds that the Lord is not yet here.

The Church is called to be vigilant with the loving watchfulness that the heart of the beloved has in vigil:

"I was sleeping, but my heart kept vigil;
I heard my lover knocking . . ." (Song 5:2).

The parable of the ten virgins speaks to us about the delay in the Lord's coming. All went out with their lamps to welcome the groom, all became drowsy and fell asleep until a cry announced his coming. Five of them were foolish and had not brought oil for their lamps. Five were wise: their lamps were filled with oil, a symbol of hope and vigilance. While the foolish ones went to find some oil, the groom arrived; ". . . those who were ready went into the wedding feast with him. Then the door was locked" (Matt 25:10).

Do we take seriously the need to be ready?

This warning applies not only to each individual but also to the entire Christian community. This is why Jesus said to his disciples, "Therefore, stay awake, for you know neither the day nor the hour" (Matt 25:13).

Let us not put off faith, hope, and love

To keep one's lamp lighted is also to grasp the Lord's warning to the Church: "Yet I hold this against you: you have lost the love you had at first" (Rev 2:4), *and* to lend an ear to his call: "Behold, I stand at the door and knock. If anyone hears my voice and opens the door, I will enter his house and dine with him, and he with me" (Rev 3:20).

43

We believe in the Holy Spirit, the Lord and giver of life

Who is the Holy Spirit?

We often turn to the Father or to Jesus. But what about the Spirit? We cannot believe in the Father and in the Son without believing in the Spirit in the same way: "With the Father and the Son he is worshiped and glorified," states the Creed.

The Spirit is itself God. It has its own personhood and own way of acting in the world and in history. It is the breath of life. After the resurrection it makes Jesus present. It upholds believers, instructs them, and introduces them to the entire truth; it is their defender, their support against persecution.

The Holy Spirit does not send us to itself. It makes us love Jesus and turns us toward the Father; it puts us into relationships with one another, for it is the source of communion. With the Father and the Son it creates the universe and cooperates in human salvation.

We proclaim that *the Holy Spirit is the Lord* and *Giver of life,* for that Spirit is truly the Spirit of the Risen Lord.

"In the name of the Father, and of the Son, and of the Holy Spirit"

The invocation of the Father, the Son, and the Holy Spirit, accompanied by the sign of the cross, begins every Christian prayer. Our prayer is made in the faith that we declare *in* the Father, the Son, and the Holy Spirit. And just as at the end of any meaningful conversation we feel the need to say "thank you," we give glory to the Father who gives us his Son, to the Son who gives himself to everyone, and to the Holy Spirit who lives in us and enables us to know the Father and the Son.

Glory to the Father,
and to the Son,
and to the Holy Spirit:
As it was in the beginning,
is now, and will be forever. Amen.

We are not merely outside observers of this relation that unites the three Persons in one God. We are also their dwelling, and we live in the midst of their relation:

"Whoever loves me . . . my Father will love him, and we will come to him and make our dwelling with him" (John 14:23).

It is also the Spirit who prays in us and makes us say "Father," even though we are not worthy to be called his children.

After Jesus' death the apostles returned home to hide their disappointment. After the resurrection the Lord promised them the Spirit. Pentecost was a liberating upheaval for the Church: the gift of the Spirit gave the early Church the strength to confront fear and doubt. It was accompanied by astonishing signs (conversions, miracles . . .), but also by more subtle signs, such as joy, communal love, and courage in the face of persecution.

What was the experience of the first Christian community?

The Spirit is a permanent gift to the Church. It sends the Risen Jesus to us and reminds us of everything the Lord told us (John 14:26).

At Pentecost the apostles were surrounded by people from many different regions. The fact that each one understood them in his or her own language is a sign that the Church calls everyone to itself. All peoples are gathered together in Christ. This event is the beginning of the Church's mission: an irresistible energy transformed a handful of people who had been devastated by Jesus' death into messengers who joyously faced all the perils of their mission.

In each of the apostles new gifts sprang up for announcing salvation: the gift of languages, the gift of healing, and many others. The most spectacular were not necessarily the most important. If the different gifts generated competition among Christians, then they ceased to be gifts from God. Their aim was misplaced if they no longer served to unite. That was the game played by the divisive spirit always at work in the world and the Church.

In what do we find the work of the Spirit?

". . . the fruit of the Spirit is love, joy, peace, patience, kindness, generosity, faithfulness . . ." (Gal 5:22).

Without doubt the work of the Spirit is most often silent, but it reveals itself in an amazing way in the courage of martyrs and in the Church's capacity for renewal, whatever its historical crises or the regimes it has had to endure.

Through baptism and confirmation we have become the Spirit's dwelling and the leaven in the dough. It is through the Spirit that God is truly with us, ". . . closer to us than we are ourselves" (St. Augustine); yet it is also through him that God acts in history. The Spirit blows where it will (John 3:8). It acts in the Church through the Word of God and

"Do not quench the Spirit"
(1 Thess 5:19).

the sacraments but also speaks through every person of good will, renewing both the face of the earth and the inner person:

Come, Holy Spirit . . .
Heal our wounds, our strength renew,
on our dryness pour your dew,
wash the stains of guilt away.
Bend the stubborn heart and will,
melt the frozen, warm the chill,
guide the steps that go astray.
(Sequence of Pentecost)

"He spoke through the prophets."

The prophet speaks for God. From the beginning, the Spirit has been speaking to human hearts, in creation and in events, in human consciousness, and in the history of the people in whom God raised up Abraham, Moses, David, and so many prophets. But the heart of God's people hardened: they were not ready to live in accordance with the Covenant. The kings put their confidence in wealth and their trust in arms. Worship was a lie: God was offered incense and the poor were exploited, sold for a pair of sandals! The law became a weight to be thrown off . . . (Amos 2:6).

To this stiff-necked and hardhearted People, the prophets announced a New Covenant (Jer 31:31). They appealed for justice, but they could not accomplish it: that was to be the task of the coming Messiah. God was preparing and sanctifying his People. He spoke of a spirit that would come into their hearts: "I will give you a new heart and place a new spirit within you" (Ezek 36:26-27). It was within this line of prophets that Jesus, filled with the Holy Spirit, would be recognized as the Word of God made flesh.

He speaks to us in Sacred Scripture.

The biblical books were written over a period of centuries. Even though this tradition employed the language of its culture, it was the product of Israel's faith and the work of the Spirit.

We say that all Scripture is holy and "inspired." That means that the authors of these books wrote because God had chosen them and had put them under the movement (inspiration) of the Spirit. Nonetheless, each one wrote within his talents and limits, conforming to various literary genres, within the mentality and culture of his own time. These human words are at the same time God's Word.

46

Day after day the Church draws from Sacred Scripture as from a fountain. There it finds grace and courage for prayer, struggle, and pardon. In the Scriptures, the Holy Spirit tells us, "Today . . . harden not your hearts" (Ps 95:8). And it sanctifies us as we listen to the Word in faith.

"O, that today you would hear his voice."

Christians, therefore, have an interpreter who makes Scripture alive and relevant for them. It is the Holy Spirit, about whom Jesus proclaimed, "He will teach you everything . . . that I told you" (John 14:26). Without the Holy Spirit, Scripture would be a dead letter and the Church would have no soul.

How does the Spirit make tradition "alive"?

The tradition received from the apostles is followed in the Church through the Spirit's life-giving action. It is better perceived and understood because the people of God live it, study it, and meditate on it in their hearts (Luke 2:19, 51),

47

and because it is transmitted by those who, as successors of the apostles, have received a "certain charism of truth" (*Dei Verbum*, 8). The Spirit, then, takes the Church along the path toward the fullness of truth.

How does the community respond to the Holy Spirit's call?

Through their love of the gospel, Christians are called to understand all the signs that express the needs and aspirations of men and women today. The Spirit teaches us to recognize and discern the signs that God provides for us in history and to respond with faith, hope, and charity. The life of Cardinal Joseph Cardijn was a striking example of this attention to the signs of the times. "Observe, judge, act," he said. He awoke in every worker's child the awareness of his or her dignity as a child of God!

Isn't it in the Holy Spirit that we discern the "signs of the times"?

The "signs of the times" are events in which Christians discern, in the light of faith, an announcement of the Kingdom to come. These signs reveal the presence of Christ in our midst. The Spirit makes us understand and unveils for us his presence in every kind deed, in every act of justice, in every cry of suffering and distress. History is filled with the presence of Christ. Yet it is always set upon by contrary forces. It is by faith that the believer can see the intervention of the Spirit in the course of events: changes in society; scientific discoveries, especially in biology; technical advances; economic crises; aspirations for justice; advancement of women; phenomena of sects; Judeo-Christian, Islamic-Christian, or Christian-Marxist dialogues; unemployment among youth; North-South or East-West dialogue.

All these developments are important, and they should be considered on the basis of their historical, social, economic, and scientific reality; yet they are not always reducible to the terms in which the sciences approach them. It is every person's right and moral duty to determine what is good and what is evil in the light of his or her conscience. The Holy Spirit acts in every person of good will who forms his or her conscience and obeys it. Christian faith clarifies everything in a new way and directs our intelligence toward solutions that respond fully to God's will concerning the human vocation.

Come, Holy Spirit . . .

Come, Holy Spirit,
fill the hearts of your faithful
and enkindle in them the fire of your love.
Send forth your Spirit and they will be created,
and you will renew the face of the earth.

Lord, you instruct your faithful
by the light of the Holy Spirit.
Grant by the same Spirit
that we may be truly wise
and ever rejoice in his consolation.

We believe in the Church

"Jesus Christ, yes! The Church, no!"

Many people today want to hold fast to the person of Jesus, a prophet in word and deed. But the Church . . . ? Doubts, disappointments, hurts, the apparent gap between the Church and Christ, the burden of rites, ambiguities, compromises with power and money, the hierarchy, and people called "faithful" when they barely are—so many trials and weaknesses, but also so many intransigent viewpoints and judgments block the discovery of the Church's true nature. The Church is at once visible and invisible, human and divine, a Church of the earth, yet rich in heavenly things.

Do we know the Church?

"If I observed you day and night," says the poet, "if I followed you wherever you went, if I could penetrate the core of your thoughts and your heart, I would still not know you: I would not know you to the extent that I did not love you."

Love the Church? Love it before coming to any conclusions about it? It is the Church that throughout the centuries, has carried us in the faith and has given us birth in joy and pain. It is the Church that has nourished us. Why do we grow up in its bosom with ingratitude or indifference?

Love the Church, since Christ has loved it and gave himself up for it; love the Church as Christ loves it today, and work so that it might be as he wants it to be.

Who can tell Christ's love for his Church?

God, says the Bible, loves us like a mother who never forgets her nursling and cares tenderly for the fruit of her womb (Isa 49:15-16). He loves us like a father who, deeply moved at the return of his son, runs toward him, embraces him, and covers him with kisses (Luke 15:20).

Yet between Christ and his Church there exists a more mysterious love that brings us into the heart of intimacy with God: it is the love of the Groom for the Bride:

"On that day, says the Lord,
she shall call me 'My husband.' . . .
I will espouse you in right and in justice,
in love and in mercy;
I will espouse you in fidelity,
and you shall know the Lord" (Hos 2:18, 21-22).

The Church lives a life of "faith in the Son of God who has loved [her] and gave himself for [her]" (Gal 2:20). This nuptial love is infinitely personal. It is strong and full of delicacy. It shines from the Bride's [Church's] face.

50

Well and good, we might say! But in reality? Above all, the Church knows that it is loved by Christ, and that alone makes it radiant: it is the sign of God's love and justice.

Jesus was not alone. Born a Jew, he belonged to a people shaped by a tradition, that of the Covenant that God had established—not with individuals but with a people. Jesus announced on the banks of the Jordan that the Kingdom of God *is here.* This Kingdom is not purely spiritual and invisible. It manifests itself in a renewed and gathered people, the sign of another world that has already begun.

Did Christ want a Church? Isn't it just an invention of some people after his death?

Jesus chose the Twelve from among his disciples. Twelve is a number that symbolizes a totality, just as Jacob's twelve sons prefigured the totality of the Chosen People: the twelve tribes of Israel.

The fact that there are twelve apostles announces figuratively the gathering of all people, for in Jesus salvation is announced to all. Among the Twelve, Peter receives from Jesus—and not from men—the responsibility of "strengthening his brethren" in the faith. Jesus established him as a rock of unity: "You are Peter [Rock] and upon this rock I will build my Church, and the gates of the netherworld shall not prevail against it" (Matt 16:18).

What is the significance of the disciples?

In Judaism and in other religions, it is the disciple who chooses to seek out a master. Between Jesus and his disciples things are otherwise. It is Jesus who calls. His call is free and unexpected, but it is so impressive that he elicits a free, total, and unconditional attachment to his person. This call causes breaks with previous conditions of life, since his disciples have not been chosen for their own sakes, but to be sent: *apostle* means "one who is sent."

We must look beyond Jesus to see the Church.

The Church, as Jesus wished, is the "one" for whom he died. ". . . Jesus was going to die for the nation—and not only for the nation, but also to gather into one the dispersed children of God" (John 11:51-52). To gather: not just into an unformed and uniform mass, but into a people composed of different persons, each unique in God's eyes. "Church," *ekklesia* in Greek, means "assembly called together." The Church is called together by God in the unity of the Spirit. God wanted it to be in his image and likeness: a community of love and persons just like God himself. He wanted it that way and gives it to us: the Trinity—one God in the communion of Persons—effects that likeness, for it is its source. The Church has its origin and source in the Trinity. The more it radiates this giant mystery of love, of

52

mutual respect and of communion, the more the sense of the Trinity will be familiar to us, and will in some way envelop us.

The Church is to be built with everybody, particularly those who are sick, who are refugees, the poor or lost, i.e., the most destitute. At first sight, there seems to be nothing there for us. In reality, these destitute are given to us by Christ as to his brothers and sisters, and it is through them that we have access to Christ. Even materially wealthy people often suffer from another poverty: that of having nothing to give and nothing to receive.

The communion between rich and poor is essential for the Church as the people whom God assembles from men and women of all ages, all social conditions, and all races: persons who normally would never be "brethren" unless they were indeed children of the one Father.

The Christian family is, in the image of the Trinity, a community of different persons. This is why the Second Vatican Council looks upon it as a "little Church," the Church in the home. Its vocation is to be an abode of love, an open community, a sign of the Kingdom in a fragmented world

Where is the mystery of the Church lived out?

53

where so many men, women, children, and elderly people suffer loneliness and lack of affection. United by the grace of the sacrament of marriage, spouses know that God's own love is communciated to them so that, in the midst of the difficulties of daily life, they can give witness to the power of him who unites them. Like the great Church, the "little Church" takes part in the ministry of evangelization.

In each diocese, the Church becomes a communion of all the communities within it and around their Shepherd: Christ, made present in the bishop. Many say, "Why is an intermediary needed between God and human beings?" But the Church is not an intermediary: it is the living Body of Christ!

How did the Church become aware of its mystery?

It was by living through actual situations (missionary expansion, brotherly love, divisions, heresies, persecutions . . .) that the apostles and evangelists spoke of the Church as a mystery revealed in Christ—one that no image could totally express: the Church is at the same time the Lord's Vine, the Bride of Christ, the Body of Christ, the Temple of the Holy Spirit, the Heavenly City.

Why does the same word—church—stand for both a people and building?

The church building is, in a manner of speaking, an image of the Church of which we are the "living rocks." Consecrated to God, just like the baptized people, it belongs to him. This building, issuing from the creativity of a believing people and dwelt in by the Body of Christ, expresses a mystery that the poor understand. Indeed, the community itself constitutes the veritable "Temple of the Holy Spirit": this people, constantly drawn together by God to hear his Word and to give thanks in the Eucharist, is sent forth into the world to be a sign there of the divine presence. Thus the church building becomes a sign of God's presence in the village or city parish.

How was the Church born?

The Church has its roots in the message of Jesus. The disciples are the nucleus around which the "new people" can gather. When Christ died, God confirmed the mission of his Son and the faith of the disciples by the resurrection of Jesus and by the gift of the Spirit.

In light of this new event the apostles, scattered by Jesus' death, reassembled. From that moment on, they formed the "Christian" community founded upon Christ who had died and risen.

54

Starting with the Jerusalem community that had witnessed Easter and Pentecost, the Church began to develop. It would soon come to feel the pain of its transformation from Jewish assembly to Christian assembly. Born of the baptism of the Spirit, the Church formed the New Israel, which gathered together all those who accepted themselves as being saved by Christ. To this day, it holds with great respect and continuing gratitude the Chosen People to whom God had entrusted the promises, the Scriptures, and the hope of the human race.

Peter and the apostles are always among us. They are the bishops, united with the presiding pope, the bishop of Rome: Peter among his brothers in the episcopacy. The bishops are not alone. Like Jesus, they shepherd the people. They live within a people and are at their service. Around each of them, from generation to generation, are the priests who share in the grace of the bishop's priesthood. Bishops

Bishops, priests, deacons, and laypeople: what roles do they perform in the Church?

55

and priests share together in the priesthood of Christ, for there is but one Priest, Christ, of whom they are the sign.

Care for the poor has marked the Church since its birth. For this reason the apostles instituted the diaconate, i.e., deacons ("servants"), whose mission is to look closely after the care of the needy, who hope in the love of the Church.

Thus the hierarchy—bishops, priests, and deacons—is not above the people of God but within this people and at its service. In the Christian community laypeople have been specifically called to give witness to the Kingdom in the world. Wherever the gospel is expected to take root (the world of the family, of work, leisure, health, study, of politics), they are called to make known the new life given by God.

Bishops, priests, and deacons—called "ordained" ministers because they have received the sacrament of holy orders— and laity are all essentially equal among the people of God. Indeed, although baptism confers the same dignity on all Christians, there are numerous distinct roles within the Church.

We believe in one Church

The Church frees us from individualism.

The Church is *already* what it is called to be because it is assembled by God in the very unity of the Father, the Son, and the Holy Spirit. At the same time, the Church is not yet completely one.

What is the role of the Eucharist in this unity?

The Church is on its way toward ultimate unity because the Holy Spirit "works" in it and sustains it as it moves forward. We say that the Church is one because it is the Body of Christ; in the Eucharist, the assembly communicates with the Lord's Body and Blood. The unifying force is not in the assembly but in Christ. When the Christian community gathers, the Eucharist is the source and foundation of the Church's unity, since it is Christ who calls the people together.

Does unity interfere with diversity?

Even in the first century, the Church did not always distinguish itself through unity! Christians were divided by partisan spirits and personal pride, and St. Paul addressed them by comparing the Church with the human body. In the body there is a diversity of members and organs (1 Cor 12:12-30). All contribute to making up the body. What would become

56

of the body if everything were ear . . . or hand? In the same way, the diversity of the Spirit's gift does not impede unity. *Diversity is richness.* It enables the whole body to live from the exchange, communication, and mutual dependence of its members. Yet the Church is not merely compared to a body; it *is* the Body of Christ! "Is Christ divided?" asked St. Paul (1 Cor 1:13).

There is a strong temptation to compare the Church with a state and to view it only as a hierarchical society in which unity is understood mainly in organizational terms. In that way the Church appears as a centralized society, its unity depending on authority exercised from the top down: the pope over bishops, then over priests, then finally over the laity. This idea of unity prevailed especially during the time when the Church had to define itself as an independent society in order to free itself from subservience to civil power.

To really understand the nature of the Church, one must begin with its inner workings; *it is a communion between God and humanity* and *among human beings.* This unity, even allowing for diversity, is achieved first of all in the local Church (the diocese), for in it, the one Church of God is fully realized. The diocese is not merely a part of the Church—like a piece in a puzzle—with all that implies of being incomplete and subordinate to the whole.

Rather, the diocese is a Church in itself, a full portion of the entire people of God, having all the characteristics of the whole Body of Christ. This is why the early Christians spoke of the Church of God that is at Corinth or at Ephesus, for example, as one would refer today to the Church of God in New York or in Chicago or Los Angeles.

The unity of the entire Church is realized in the communion of all the local churches among themselves in union with Peter's successor, the pope. This unity is all the more glorious because each local church is marked by the diversity of the Christians who make it up.

God calls upon his believers to form only one people. Ecumenism is the movement toward reconciliation, a movement prompted by the Holy Spirit among the various Christian Churches separated by historical conflicts and misunderstandings. The various separated Churches continually search for this unity in the Body of Christ.

What is ecumenism?

The desire for unity is both a call and a gift of God to the Church. It does not suppress the diversity of sentiment within the one apostolic tradition that Christians have in common.

Why hasn't ecumenism advanced more rapidly?

To be reconciled does not mean "to make it look as if there were no differences." It takes more than thirty years to neutralize several centuries of separation and misunderstanding that have caused our Churches to develop along lines of distrust and sometimes even rivalry. The reconciliation of Christians cannot be carried out by disregarding truth, but the longing for mutual understanding and brotherly collaboration is clearly one of the greatest graces of this century. Ecumenism advances in step with the conversion of each of us to Christ and his gospel.

How can we foster ecumenism?

Every split in the Body of Christ is an injury. However, it is an injury that Christ can heal; it is not fatal. Every year—from January 18 to 25, the Churches observe a week of prayer for Christian unity, an intensive period of prayer, meetings, and celebrations among Christians of different Churches throughout the world. It is the source and summit of our continuous efforts toward reconciliation.

We may also unite in promoting social peace and extending aid to the needy, thus rendering witness by jointly trying to practice Christian charity. Sharing in Eucharistic communion, however, the fruit of unity, is not condoned as a means for achieving unity.

58

We believe in the holy Church

Because sinners—and we are *all* sinners—remain genuine members of the Church, even in sin, our sin affects the whole Church; the entire Body of Christ suffers accordingly; the whole Temple of the Spirit is shaken by it. The Church is not "holy" merely in the sense of being "above" our sinful condition, for it is itself a communion of sinners. God's holiness shines forth and touches all who turn to him. In the New Testament this call to holiness can only be understood in terms of Jesus, "the holy One of God" (Mark 1:24). Christ sacrificed himself so that men and women could be saints (John 17:19). Holiness is not the result of our moral or religious behavior by itself. It is the work of God who makes us holy. The holiness that the Spirit gives us in baptism is a gift not only to each one of us; it is the entire people that has entered into the Covenant with God by the Blood of Christ. In him, God is bound to sinners; through his Spirit, he has made his people out of "those who were not [a] people" (Rom 9:25). All the sins of the world cannot thwart the divine plan for the sanctification of the Church.

Isn't the Church made up of sinners?

Let us not be afraid to say along with St. Paul that the members of the Church are saints because of the holiness of God who has saved and loved them. This holiness never turns us in upon ourselves, for it is a grand opening up to God, to the world, and to others. The Church is holy, too, because it is the Bride of Christ with whom it has become as one. Purified by the Blood of Christ and by baptismal waters, we are continually refreshed and restored by the Eucharist and the reconciliation that it effects; for it is the Eucharist that helps us resemble the Lord.

Why do we believe that the Church is holy?

59

What is the communion of saints?	Since the Church's earliest years, Christians have prayed for the dead and offered the Eucharist for the departed; they also pray to the saints and ask for their help. This mutual love and spiritual exchange reconciles and unites us. This is what we call "the communion of saints." The dead are close to us because they are close to Christ. It is in the Eucharist that we find them along with Mary, the apostles, and all the saints, since it is there that we are in communion with him through whom they are living.
Can I help others with my prayer?	The communion of saints unites all the members of the Body of Christ, those of yesterday and those of today, in heaven and from one end of the earth to another. Thus even the most abandoned people know that they are never completely alone, and those who suffer know that the offering of their life benefits the entire Body of Christ. Those who are dying know that the Church accompanies them in death and waits for them in Christ's glory. Therefore, in our homes and hospitals, the sick are often better at praying than those who have, by vocation, dedicated their whole lives to prayer. Those who sow the gospel in pain and who harvest it in song know that they owe their courage, their joy in the faith, and the effectiveness of their mission to the whole Body of Christ.
Holiness of a child of God	God wills the sanctification of all men and women because they are all called to be his children and to share in his holiness. Even though we do not always heed God's call, God understands us when we pray, "Forgive us our trespasses, as we forgive those who trespass against us." For our holiness as children of the Father is mainly that of repentant children.
Holiness has many faces!	Holiness takes many forms in the daily life of Christians. Many men and women feel called to proclaim the gospel, and religious orders and youth groups have been created to serve this inclination. Others see despair in the world and feel compelled to bring about Christian hope in its midst. They seek to liberate, visit, console, and help the oppressed, the imprisoned, the afflicted, and the deprived. Many Christians get involved in movements for peace and justice, for human rights, and so forth. The Spirit pours out countless graces for many different people, whose lives are sustained by the incomparable charity that it places in our hearts. All people are called to dutifully assume their political and social responsibilities. The Spirit also opens their eyes to the need for love and human warmth in society.

Some families open their homes to those who suffer various kinds of distress; others gather in community to share and to give of themselves entirely in following Christ.

Obedience to the Spirit creates different spiritual families: Throughout history, men and women who hear the same call to action or to contemplation have tended to group together in a common bond. Thus the Church has been able to regard changing situations and world needs through the eyes of many different men, women, and young people, resulting in an abundance of Christian spiritual styles that mutually enrich each other.

What is spirituality?

The task of discerning the work of the Spirit in every situation belongs to everyone, but particularly to bishops: "Do not quench the Spirit. . . . Test everything; retain what is good" (1 Thess 5:19, 21).

We believe in the catholic Church

The word "Catholic" is not in opposition to Protestant, Orthodox, or Anglican. *Catholic* means "universal." The Church is catholic, or it does not exist. Since its birth on Pentecost, it has been open to every race, language, people, and nation. The Book of the Acts of the Apostles takes pleasure in citing all the newcomers: Parthians, Medes, Elamites . . . they come from everywhere. That small band of Galileans, the original apostles, are tremendously outnumbered; by virtue of their preaching, the Spirit's fire has reached the four corners of the world.

Why would it ever bother us to say we are Catholics?

If the Church is not catholic, it is no more than a group withdrawn into itself or a party of people who assemble because they are alike. But the Church that God raises up is called to open itself to all and to become the community of all human beings in Christ.

To be "catholic": a gift of the Spirit

To be catholic is to have an attitude of openness, not an attitude of withdrawal into self, into one's outlook, into one's customs or ways of thinking. It means to have, in the name of the gospel, a passion to be concerned about everybody, whatever their mentality, their milieu, or their culture, since we know that the Good News is destined for all humanity. We live out this passion in fraternal communion with all the Churches.

One is not catholic simply by wishing it! To have a heart burning with faith, hope, and charity for all, not for just those around us, is a gift of the Spirit. However, people do not baptize themselves; this is a gift conferred through another upon every Christian. It is through baptism that one shares in the mission of the Church sent by the Lord "to all nations."

Where there are small, lively communities, what purpose do parishes serve?

Organizing the Church into dioceses and parishes allows Christians of every social status and persuasion to come together in a place open to everyone. All interest groups and organized movements are called upon to gather there and cooperate in making this an open area. All parishes are called to share a mutual concern for each other and for all the Churches.

We believe in the apostolic Church

When we proclaim that the Church is "apostolic," we affirm that everything that is essential in it goes back to Christ through the apostles. Even today we live in timeless communion with the apostles on all continents. This fidelity is guaranteed by the apostolic succession of the pastors, but it is also maintained by the whole people of God united with its pastors: from generation to generation they confess the faith of the apostles in doctrine, sacraments, and life.

Is the Church faithful to its origins?

If the Church has such a great concern for the purity of the faith and for a deepening of it, it is because fidelity to the apostles' preaching is the guarantee that the Church is the Church of Christ.

Do we try to understand our faith?

The apostles exercised real authority over the Church. Paul wrote his epistles to explain the faith correctly, but also to provide directives that deal with the concrete behavior of Christians. To this day, the Church's apostolic authority is carried on by the successors to the apostles.

Does the Church have authority over conscience?

The mission of the pope and the bishops is to ensure that the Church truly remain an organized body, where everything is done for the good of all. The role of the diocesan

bishops, collectively and individually, is not limited to interpreting the faith correctly for the faithful. The bishops also insure that the faithful act and live in communion with one another in order to build the Church.

This real authority over consciences is used with great care. The bishop, more than others, must be attentive to the signs of the times and be concerned about the way the Church's faithful live. This authority of the pastors is itself carried out in obedience to the Word of God.

Are the "precepts of the Church" still in force?

Is one free to practice his or her faith guided only by individual conscience? Christians live out their faith along with others in their witness for justice, in prayer, and through participation in rites and sacraments. These gatherings are "strong times" of conversion; they are the means by which the Church is made visible, and its members strengthen their faith *as a community*.

It is in this sense that Catholic tradition gives us the "Precepts of the Church" as so many invitations to be transformed together. They are:

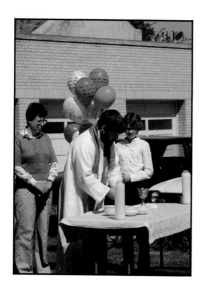

- to assist at Mass on Sundays and holy days of obligation and rest from servile labor on Sunday and the holy days.

- to observe the laws of fast and abstinence on the days appointed by the Church.

- to confess one's sins at least once a year.

- to receive the Eucharist at least once a year during the Easter season.

- to support the pastor and the Church according to one's means.

- to observe the marriage laws of the Church.

These precepts are instructions for living: they challenge and stimulate us personally to "build the Church." In the life of the community, our place is unique and our witness irreplaceable.

We often hear "This declaration is insupportable." "That I cannot accept." . . . Before asking ourselves if everything the pope and the bishops say is true and unalterable, it is good to ask ourselves how much confidence we place in the successors of the apostles.

One who believes and trusts in the Church takes to heart the teaching of the bishops and the pope regarding faith and morals when they speak to the Church as pastors; this is called their "ordinary ministry."

Through the apostles and their successors, we are in touch with the living tradition of the gospel by virtue of a real authority. The pope and the bishops are not sent by men but by Christ. They benefit from the Spirit of him who sends them. It is in the same Spirit that the faithful understand their teaching. The Church in its entirety is assured of not being abandoned by God. This assurance that "the community of the faithful," having been anointed by the Lord, cannot be deceived regarding the faith (*Lumen Gentium* 12) is what tradition calls the "infallibility" of the Church.

Jesus said to the one he named "Peter," that is, "Rock": "I have prayed that your own faith may not fail; and once you have turned back, you must strengthen your brothers" (Luke 22:32). If the pope receives "in a singular way the charism of infallibility that belongs to the Church herself" (*Lumen Gentium* 25), he does not receive it as a private person. He is assured of infallibility when he speaks *ex cathedra,* that is, "from his chair" as successor of Peter, as pastor and teacher of all the faithful, to strengthen the community in the faith. By virtue of his apostolic responsibility, he then proclaims definitively a point of doctrine relating to faith and morals. Infallibility belongs equally to the college of bishops when, along with and under the authority of the pope, an ecumenical council defines one or another point of faith and morals.

The pope does not enjoy the assistance of the Holy Spirit in revealing new doctrines, but in unity with the bishops, he protects and expounds the revelation transmitted by the apostles.

How could God abandon his Church?

What is papal infallibility?

We look for the resurrection of the dead and the life of the world to come

Merely waiting for something is too easy!

To wait for something means to look forward to it. We look forward to the resurrection; that is what we dare to hope. Everything in the Creed would be meaningless if there were no resurrection. How could God be the Creator, Lord, and Savior of humanity if humanity had to disappear forever?

Our faith resolutely orients us toward the future. This is not an empty future because, thanks to a gift of God that is yet to come, we are destined to enter, through death, into full communion with him who makes us live.

Such a future is something all the saints have ardently desired. Through this desire they neither avoided the present nor denied history. They gave to men and women an awareness of their true dignity, a dignity that flourishes beyond death. Since apostolic times Christians have testified to their faith by belief in the resurrection of the dead.

Is it Christian to neglect one's body?

It is because of their faith that Christians attach importance to the human body. God fashioned us a body "out of the clay of the ground" and quickened it with "the breath of life" (Gen 2:7). In his Son he took the flesh of our humanity, was born of a woman, and suffered blows and injuries; after the resurrection, he showed himself bodily alive.

The body is inseparable from the person and is an integral part of it. It is through the body that a human being receives the sacraments and communicates with the Body of Christ, with brothers and sisters, and the whole world. The body is holy as is the person: it comes from God and it goes to God. Respect for the body is respect for the person.

That is why our Christian faith urges us to take care of those who suffer or who are despised in their bodies. In this manner, for example, Father Damien's love for lepers made him like them in everything, at a time when contracting leprosy was signing one's own death warrant.

What meaning does the resurrection have for contemporary life?

We are certainly not the only ones to comfort the suffering. Nevertheless, we are inspired by a hope that is especially ours and that makes us say, "My body will live because I will live. My body has, right from this moment, embarked upon an adventure through time and eternity."

66

It is by this faith in creation and resurrection that the Christian respects his or her body and that of the infant already conceived. Christians are called upon to make gifts of their lives, in gladness or suffering, in natural death or in martyrdom, because they are buoyed by the joyful hope that no trial, not even death, will separate them from the love of Christ (Rom 8:38).

To believe in resurrection, it is necessary to accept dying, and truly dying, as Christ did. Christ died in the full reality of his humanity. He did not survive of his own accord as someone who owed nothing to anyone. In his death as a man, he placed his life in the Father's hands, and God raised him up.

Is survival the same as resurrection?

To survive means to endure, i.e., "not to die" but to continue to live on one's own. But it is by *grace* that *we are raised*. To be raised again is to gain back one's entire being—body and soul—from God.

Many allow themselves to be captivated—in the true sense of the word—by belief in reincarnation. After death, people

And reincarnation?

67

are said to pursue their existence in other lives until at some point they enter into a state called "nirvana." In this view of reality, life offers nothing unique or definitive: it does not promise eternity forthwith. It is only a phase in a cycle in which one is born and reborn, conditioned by one's previous life, until the final purification. This belief is incompatible with Christian faith.

Does purgatory exist? In the face of the mystery of death, which we little understand, the majority of people feel, perhaps vaguely, the need to be purified. This is why many offer sacrifices, plead with divinities, submit to rituals, or seek out means to purify (purge) themselves through asceticism or meditation before the great rendezvous with death.

This desire for purification is something that God has implanted in the human heart. Such a desire has to be Christianized. The Christian knows that his or her love for God and neighbor is imperfect and must be healed by Christ's love.

Punishment or purification? God answers this Christian desire for healing through his mercy. Purification after death does not happen according to our notion of time and place. It is a state in which God's love totally consumes whatever is blocking us from being completely happy in his presence.

Does hell exist? Hell is a state in which a person consciously and deliberately refuses all communication with God and other people. Hell exists because it is possible for people to allow themselves to be captivated by their pride. Hell is the consequence of refusing grace—God's mercy.

People do not enter into the presence of God by their own means; rather, God, by his grace and love, admits them into his presence. If a person refuses such an invitation, God judges that refusal. This is why, in Scripture, hell involves an aspect of punishment.

The Word and Mary Mary received the Word in her heart and provided a human body for the Son of God. God loved her with a special love and associated her "body and soul" with his Son's death and resurrection. In her the Church contemplates its own future. This is the mystery we celebrate on August 15, the feast of the Assumption of the Blessed Virgin Mary.

Where is humanity going? The love that we have for God and for one another does not vanish at the moment of death but is preserved through Christ, who lives with the Father. Thus when human beings die, we remain in communion with them because they are living in the Father's love. The dead keep their relation of love with us and they wait for us with Christ in the "New Jerusalem." The gospel speaks to us about a family life around God, about a banquet to which we are invited, about a face-to-face vision of God. As for us, our resurrection has already begun, says St. Paul, because the Spirit of the Risen One gives us life. But it is not yet apparent.

Living in Christ, the dead already have a share in his resurrection. However, we await the resurrection of all on the "last day," because the whole human community is not yet reunited in the full growth of the Body of Christ.

Purification of the dead implies a suffering that is rooted in love. The dead who suffer from not being able to receive the gift of God depend upon our oneness with them and our prayers so that they might be healed of the consequences of their sins and might blossom into communion with God.

In the gospel, health, peace, justice, and mercy announce the coming of the Kingdom of God. Commitment to justice and to the transformation of society and of its structures is essential for the Church. Yet its mission is not confined to the social and political aspects of history. The Church is *in* the world and *for* the world. Yet is is also on its way *toward* "the Jerusalem on high."

Where there is Christ, there is the Church: the Risen Christ is among us, but his glorious presence transcends time and space. The earthly Church moves through history in communion with the heavenly Church, already assembled in Christ's glory.

Living and struggling in the world, we are united in common love and praise with a Church we have yet to experience. This union is a special joy to us that sustains the fervor of our hope. Our love for human beings demands more of ourselves because we know that we are "citizens of heaven" and that our home is "in heaven."

"God is preparing for us a new dwelling and a new earth, where justice will reign and happiness will fulfill and surpass all the desires for peace that surge in the human heart" (*Gaudium et Spes*, 39). *Henceforth* we are preparing ourselves to receive this gift of God.

Do the dead already share in the resurrection?

69

Amen!

"Body of Christ." "Amen!" Such a short word! Gregorian chant reached a point of stretching this acclamation over so many notes that one had to breathe twice in order to reach the end.

"Amen!" "Amen!" Is there any other word more empty of meaning? Doesn't it betray an impatience to end talk that has gone on too long? To say "amen" to someone, to "yes" someone: The expression has become a somewhat typical and trite rejoinder.

"Amen," however, means, "yes, it is *certain,* it is *firm,* I believe that!" What is worse than not being able to rely on someone? Or being dropped by a friend? "Amen" is a miniature creed. This joyful and vigorous proclamation punctuates our celebrations and prayers. It does not mean "end point" but a responsive point: With this word, I answer that I believe. The "Amen" that concludes the Creed declares our assent to the work of the Father, the Son, and the Spirit in the Church.

It is in the act of communion with Christ that the "Amen" takes on its full meaning. By the Holy Spirit we say "yes," the "yes" of Christ. The word is accompanied by the gesture of open hands at communion, the sign of one poor in spirit; for only those who are poor in spirit can rely on someone other than themselves.

Part II

Celebrating
the Lord

Opening Ourselves to God and the World

What would love be like without lively and continual expression, at least implicit, often explicit? What would faith be like without prayer, the vital link that connects us with God? Without it, God becomes abstract, distant, and strange, somewhat the image we might have of a friend who has died.

Why pray?

In prayer Christians recognize their Creator and Savior. Every movement that turns a person toward God is inspired by the Holy Spirit. It is through God that the believer surrenders to a sense of wonder, to adoration, to praise, to supplication, to avowal of personal sin or misery, to petition for grace or forgiveness. Are not love and forgiveness as necessary to life as our daily bread?

People become adults when they are able to acknowledge their parents. They begin to acknowledge everything they have received from one person or another: by doing this they mature, blossom, and become fit for new relationships.

Praying like a child

73

The Christian's joy lies precisely in turning to the Father with a child's heart, a heart that is open and docile toward God's action. This joy is not some feeble emotion. Sometimes Christians feel unable to pray. They are in the dark night of doubt or of sin, and God seems far away. Yet they know that the Spirit dwells in them by the grace of baptism and that it does not cease to be active, despite their emptiness.

Is prayer a withdrawal?

Prayer is a free act. It makes us free and allows us to serve God and others. It changes us and thereby changes the world. People who confess no God—unless it be themselves—want to possess and dominate. Prayer fills us with the "same attitude that is also . . . in Christ Jesus" (Phil 2:5). It fortifies our love and our witness. It overwhelms us with the power of God's love for his little ones and gives us the courage to conquer the forces of evil in ourselves and in the world. The world desperately needs this tenderness and power of God. Who will open themselves to it? Those who are affected by it and glow from within.

Does God answer our prayers?

Often we say, "What does God do about injustice?" He raises up men and women, believers seized by the Spirit and able to dedicate themselves to justice, who make good use of forgiveness. From those who live prayerful lives he draws out thousands of saints and witnesses who are for the most part unknown, but who are the "leaven in the dough."

God does not always answer our prayers as we might wish, but he takes to heart everything that we experience. He is not closed to our demands. He knows better than we do what we really need, even before we ask him for it.

How do we find time to pray?

Like love, prayer requires courage—the courage to regularly interrupt one's agitated and harried course of life to give oneself "time to love," the time to love God for himself, and to let oneself be loved by God. It is not a matter of duration but of intensity, of the quality of presence.

The real issue is not trying to find the time to put God into a busy life, but of seeking how to live in a way that is intensely present to God.

Isn't private prayer just as good?

The public and common prayer of the people of God is an essential function of the Church. From the beginning, the baptized "devoted themselves to the teaching of the apostles and to the communal life, to the breaking of the bread and to the prayers" (Acts 2:42). Common prayer has

74

a special value: "For where two or three are gathered together in my name, there am I in the midst of them" (Matt 18:20).

There is much evidence that the first believers, in line with Jewish tradition, prayed at regular hours. These common prayers gradually made up the "Liturgy of the Hours," which have the purpose of sanctifying the whole day and all human activity. This uninterrupted tradition is attested by religious communities that gather together day and night to offer to God the Church's praise and supplication.

Sanctifying all of life

At different times during the day, priests pray the "Breviary," the "Liturgy of the Hours," a collection of psalms and scriptural meditations that may be prayed as well by all the people of God. In some churches, Christians gather on their way to work, during the lunch hour, or after work at five o'clock in the afternoon (Vespers) to join in this prayer of the Church.

Is the "Liturgy of the Hours" for everybody?

In society-at-large, millions of Christians celebrate the sacraments together and devote themselves to prayers that cultivate simplicity of heart: the rosary, stations of the cross, pilgrimages, processions, adoration of the Blessed Sacrament. Within the family, parents and children come to-

Some believers try to gather for prayer.

gether to share their faith by reviewing the previous Sunday's Gospel or previewing the Gospel of the Sunday to come. Sometimes friends or neighbors take part in such gatherings. Here and there numerous prayer groups come into being, or existing ones are rejuvenated. These are a beacon for those who seek the path of faith, personal prayer, and community. Personal prayer feeds upon the Church's prayer, thus opening our hearts to a universal dimension.

Personal prayer and the Church's prayer

The prayers of the baptized are offered first of all as members of the Body of Christ: whether ill and lonely, imprisoned or abandoned, whether they pray at a bus stop or on a train, in a car or in a room, the whole Church prays with them, the Church of heaven and of earth, of all places and all times—past, present, and future. What a source of confidence and jubilation to know that we are members of one and the same body, the Body of the Lord! For our prayer is the prayer of Christ, which he brings to the Father.

Morning Prayer

Holy Father,
thank you for the gift of life.
Bless this day.
Let our work and our interaction
be the seeds of your Kingdom.
May your Spirit work in us and in the world.
We ask this through Jesus Christ,
your Beloved.

Evening Prayer

Holy Father,
thank you for this day that you have given us
and for those whom we have welcomed into our lives.
Forgive us our trespasses
and our lack of caring.
Give us your mercy and peace.
"Into your hands, Lord, I commend my spirit."

Prayer Before Meals

Bless us, Lord,
and bless this meal,
fruit of the earth and work of human hands.
May this nourishment that we are about to take
make us joyful in your service
and quick to share with others.
Amen.

Prayer After Meals

We give you thanks,
Lord,
for this meal that restores our strength
and draws us closer in our love for one another.
May your love increase faith, hope, and love in us.
Amen.

To help us pray . . .

The Church's most beautiful prayer is the offering of Christ to his Father in the Eucharist. Every day, but especially on Sunday, the Church renews this mystery and asks us to participate in it by first listening to the Word of God. It is important to prepare oneself, before the Mass, to absorb this Word, for example by reading it to oneself in a missal or Bible, and to meditate on it during the week in order to make it more meaningful. We find the Word, of course, in the Bible, but when we open it, we often ask ourselves, "Where do we start?" The Church, like a mother, provides us with daily Scripture readings. She offers us a very simple way: pray with the readings of the day, uniting ourselves with Christian communities the world over, and living in the rhythm of liturgical time.

The reader will find in this book several prayers from among those that Christian tradition has favored, in particular the "Our Father." One can also enhance one's faith, hope, and love in the prayers that the Church traditionally calls "acts" of faith, hope, and love.

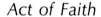

How to pray? The Church prays like Mary listening to the annunciation; who sings and proclaims her messianic joy at the visitation; who gives birth to the Word made flesh; who offers Christ to his Father at the presentation in the temple; who intercedes for men and women at Cana; who joins with her Son's offering under the cross and who, in the upstairs room, ardently awaits the coming of the Spirit along with the apostles and all the faithful. In her prayer, the Church follows the path that Mary has opened for us.

Act of Faith

I believe in you, my God,
Father, Son, and Holy Spirit.
Your Word is truth
and your law is deliverance. Your love saves
humanity and creation.
I believe in the Church
who gives us
your Word and your life.
It is the Body of Christ,
of which we are all members.
In this faith
I want to live and die.

My God, I firmly believe
everything you have revealed
and all that the holy Church presents for our belief
because you are truth itself,
and because you can neither deceive nor be deceived.
In this faith, I want to live and die.

Act of Hope

I hope in you, my God,
Father, Son, and Holy Spirit.
You have created us
in your image and likeness.
You have entrusted all creation to us.
You never abandon a man or woman in their trials and
*   temptations.*
You are kind and merciful
toward the sinner who repents.
In this hope
I want to live and die.

My God, I firmly hope that by the merits of Jesus Christ,
you will grant heaven and the graces to attain it,
because you are kind beyond measure toward us,
all-powerful and faithful in your promises.
In this hope, I want to live and die.

Act of Love

I love you, my God,
Father, Son, and Holy Spirit,
source of all love.
I love you with all my heart
and above all things,
and I love my neighbor
as myself
for love of you.
In this love
I want to live and die.

My God, I love you
above everything, with all my heart,
with all my soul, and all my strength,
because you are infinitely perfect
and lovable beyond all things.
I also love my neighbor as myself
for love of you.
In this love, I want to live and die.

Act of Contrition

Father, I have sinned against you.
It is your love that inspires me
to repent of my faults.
By the death and resurrection of your Son,
deliver me from my sins.
By the power of your Holy Spirit
I want to live firmly
in charity, truth, and justice.
In this contrition
I want to live and die.

O my God, I am heartily sorry
for having offended you.
I detest all my sins
because I dread the loss of heaven
and the pains of hell.
But most of all because they offend you,
my God, who are all good and deserving
of all my love.
I firmly resolve, with the help of your grace,
to sin no more and to avoid
the near occasions of sin.

Words and Signs of God

What would be the love of parents toward their children, friendship and community in times of trouble, the love of the engaged and the married, or care for the sick if we only had words? In the most important moments of life, whether joyful or sorrowful, words must be accompanied by actions to touch the human heart. The Church, too, has actions that "speak."

We have great need of signs

If words have the power to "touch," to wound, or to heal, it is because they are carried by a set of signs that "speak" of love and tenderness, contempt or indifference.

Words that "touch" . . .

God touches us with his Word and with his actions. The Bible says poetically that his hands fashioned us in his image. Did he not liberate his people "with a strong hand and an outstretched arm"? God touches us because he comes near us. He took on our humanity to be intimately united with us. Through Jesus' hand God heals, blesses, reconciles, and consecrates.

When God reveals himself through signs, he puts himself within our reach. He does not trample, he lifts up. The Father's most beautiful sign or indication of this is that he sent his Son. The Latin word *sacramentum* means, among other things, "a solemn oath of fidelity by means of an authentic sign." This is why we say that Jesus Christ is the sacrament above all others that makes the connection between God and human beings. The Church in its turn is the sacrament of Christ's presence among us. In the Church, each sacrament is a word and a deed of salvation. The Lord makes us reborn into a new life, confirms us, and pardons our sins; he reconciles us, unites us as bride and groom; he gathers his people at the same table and provides himself as nourishment; he cures the sick and provides us with pastors.

Is there any greater sign than Christ?

Whoever confers a sacrament must have the intention of doing what the Church intends. Even if the one conferring the sacrament is a sinner, the sacrament is not any less effective, since it is the Lord who acts through the sacramental action. Whether Peter, Paul, or Judas baptizes, "it is Christ who baptizes," says St. Augustine.

Do sacraments make a real change in a believer's life?

It is by encountering the Risen One that we are transformed. Thus the sacraments are the work of the Spirit. Thanks to

83

the Spirit, we are able to meet with the Lord through sacramental words and actions, by which he brings about our salvation and renews our existence. The encounter with the Risen One requires the faith of the one seeking the sacrament, while the faith of the Church substitutes for that of a child's at the time of his or her baptism or confirmation. Indeed, Christ himself could accomplish no saving action for someone who did not believe in him (Mark 6:5).

Could it be that our celebrations leave us with an empty feeling because our own commitment is weak? One who truly loves takes time for preparation in body and soul for the encounter with the beloved. The Christian prepares inwardly for the encounter with Christ. A celebration experienced "from within" remains without parallel for us today, tomorrow, and into the future.

How does God speak and act in the Church?

"I am with you always, until the end of the age," says the Lord (Matt 28:20).

Sometimes we ask how we can find the Risen One. Actually, he is the one who comes to us where we are. The Church, the Body of Christ, lets us perceive him in our own time. It does this by proclaiming the Word and by the sacraments of baptism, confirmation, the Eucharist, reconciliation, anointing of the sick, marriage, and holy orders.

The Lord is not only present in the Word and the sacraments but also in the assembly called together by him and in the celebrant who acts in his name.

We celebrate the Lord and also the fact of being together by virtue of the Father's call. The announcement of the Good News filled with joy those who converted and believed in the Lord. This joy of those earliest times is still ours. We do not believe "each one for oneself," but faith brings us together, just as it did for the disciples and the crowds at hearing Peter's voice on Pentecost (Acts 2:14-36). Our joy is still expressed today by songs, hymns, and psalms to celebrate God-with-us.

Did Jesus institute the seven sacraments?

Christ is present in the Eucharist, even after the celebration, under the signs of bread and wine. This is why the Holy Eucharist is reserved in the tabernacle: first that it might be carried to the sick and dying but also to enable the faithful to pray in the presence of the Blessed Sacrament. Their prayer of adoration unites them to the paschal mystery; it allows them to participate in the sacrifice of Christ, of which

84

the Eucharist is the "permanent" sacrament. One who communicates spiritually in this way or who receives the Body of Christ outside of the Eucharistic celebration, expresses a desire to share fully in the Mass.

The Eucharist is the source and summit of all Christian life. The believer's prayer is inspired and supported by the presence of Christ in our churches: "The teacher is here and is asking for you" (John 11:28). This presence makes our church the place to encounter the Lord. "The one who calls you is faithful" (1 Thess 5:24).

All the sacraments have their origin in Christ, dead and risen, who willed to share his life through these signs of his Church. That does not mean, however, that we know the place, the time, and the actual words of institution for each one of them.

As regards the Eucharist, the evangelists Matthew, Mark, and Luke, as well as St. Paul (1 Cor 11:23), give clear testimony about its institution by Jesus. As for baptism: John was baptizing before Jesus, but the Church realizes that baptism in Jesus' name is different from that of John's. "I have baptized you with water; he will baptize you with the holy Spirit" (Mark 1:8). The apostolic writings (Gospels, Epistles, Acts) give witness that baptism in Jesus' name confers the Spirit (Acts 19:1-7). They relate several times that Jesus commanded the apostles to baptize and also to forgive sins. Only God has this power, and the Risen Jesus entrusted it to the apostles.

The testimonies are not as explicit regarding the other sacraments. The apostolic writings speak of the laying on of hands upon those who are mandated for a mission, of the anointing of the sick with oil, and of Christian marriage—"mystery of Christ and the Church."

The first Christians' reflection on Jesus' deeds and actions was guided by certain events. Thus in the case of confirmation, the Church discovered that the gift of the Spirit, insofar as it confirms baptism, can be manifested by an action apart from baptism (Acts 8:14-17). As for marriage, it preexisted as an institution. However, in considering the words of Jesus on the demands of conjugal fidelity, the apostles became aware of the specific quality of Christian marriage. Jesus healed the sick and handed that mission on to the apostles. The Church has perceived in these actions of healing the body, the healing of the heart and a remis-

"[The Holy Spirit] . . . will teach you everything, and remind you of all that [I] told you" (John 14:26).

85

sion of sin as well. It is by reason of this commissioning of the Twelve and of the role of shepherd entrusted to Peter that the Church knows itself to be instituted by Jesus as an apostolic and hierarchical community.

The Church—minister of the sacraments

When the Church confesses that all the sacraments were instituted by Jesus, it does not understand this in the canonical sense. It confidently states that all the saving actions have been willed by Jesus and have their source in him. It is he himself who now baptizes and confirms and who offers himself to the Father and to human beings. He himself pardons sins. He himself anoints the sick to save them; he himself seals the conjugal union; he himself communicates his powers in ordination. He is always the one who primarily confers the sacrament. The role of the Church, then, is to be the "steward of the mysteries of God" (1 Cor 4:1): The sacraments are not its property. The Church also concludes that it cannot eliminate any of the seven sacraments and that it cannot add any others. It does not administer them as if it were their author, but the Church announces and hands on to its people the graces that come to it from Christ. Thus in all times the words and deeds of the Lord remain manifest, so that during every age men and women can answer Christ's call, take part in his paschal mystery, and share in his mission until "God may be all in all" (1 Cor 15:28; cf. Col 3:11).

"You who pass by, come near;
the source of salvation flows for you.
Behold the cross from which life springs.

Grace purifies you from all stain,
grace like a water of innocence.
Pardon yourselves, as I pardoned you.
Behold, the cross from which life springs.

My blood is shed for you,
the blood of the covenant new.
Take and drink, all you.
Behold the cross from which life springs.

My spirit I pour into your hearts,
Spirit of my love and my peace.
Bear love one for another
as I have borne my love for you.
Behold the cross from which life springs."

Chant of the Abbey of Tamié (SM K 42)

Rebirth Through Baptism

Request baptism?

Today, in our country as in others, baptisms of adults, of young people, or of school-age children are more frequent because many of them did not receive the grace of baptism immediately following their birth. Baptism is a rite that involves the whole person and confers upon that person a new life. To request it, for oneself or for one's child, is to take on a serious responsibility. This request also involves the responsibility of the whole community.

A baptism of conversion?

To receive baptism is an act of humility and of truth. The crowds who came to be baptized by John the Baptist in the Jordan were already confessing their sins. They confessed their humanity and acknowledged that they could not live their lives without help. They admitted that they were sinners and they asked for forgiveness. In doing all this, they were indeed humble.

John baptized with water to bring about a profound change of attitude. People asked him, "What should we do?" He answered them, "Whoever has two cloaks should share with the person who has none." He also said they should be honest in all their affairs, never inflict violence or harm anyone" (Luke 3:10-14). The simplicity of this response is stirring in its truthfulness. Indeed, a person who does all this does not remain the same! Yet Christian baptism does not stop there.

Why did Jesus have himself baptized?

Jesus submitted himself to John's baptism. Conceived by the Holy Spirit, born of the Virgin Mary, he lived from the time of his conception under the influence of the Holy Spirit. Yet, at the threshold of his public life, before announcing the Good News of the Kingdom, he asked for John's baptism. He thus confessed that he was truly man, in solidarity with all human beings. The reality of Christ breaks upon us with this act of humility.

As Jesus came out of the water, the Father's voice proclaimed that he was his beloved Son in whom he was well-pleased, and the Spirit descended upon Jesus. Through baptism, Jesus was therefore proclaimed Son of God, Anointed of the Spirit, Prophet, and Servant of God. From then on, Jesus belonged no longer to his family, but to his people and to all of humanity: he then began his public life.

Beyond his baptism by John, Jesus aspired to his own baptism, to his paschal mystery, to his passing over from death on the cross to resurrection from the dead. ''. . . I must be baptized, and how great is my anguish until it is accomplished!'' (Luke 12:50), he said in speaking about his death. This baptism is a baptism by blood. When an unbaptized person dies as a martyr, i.e., as a witness to faith in Jesus Christ, he or she shares in this baptism of Christ, in his paschal mystery, and will rise again with him. Jesus anxiously desired his baptism, his pasch. Unbaptized people, once they learn of the good things conferred by baptism, may also experience this desire: the grace to believe in God, to hope in God who saves us, to love God and neighbor, and to receive forgiveness for sin. If they should die while still desiring these good things, their death is a baptism of desire, and they, too, will rise with Christ. Indeed, wherever the Spirit of God breathes, the life of God also takes hold, and the person defeats sin and death. Jesus calls all

''Can you . . . be baptized with the baptism with which I must be baptized?'' (Mark 10:38, JB).

The Baptism of Jesus. Viet Stoss (late 15th c.). Polychromed and gilded wood, from an altarpiece at Cracow. Metropolitan Museum of Art, New York.

men and women to receive the baptism that he himself received. When people respond to Jesus' call and become baptized, they acknowledge their sinfulness and confess their belief in the Good News. Baptism seals the act of faith: it reveals the truth of the conversion through the humility of the candidate for baptism, i.e., a catechumen. Through a profound change of attitude, the new Christian submits to the Father's judgment: God justifies him by faith and makes him just.

Baptized in the Spirit and in fire!

"The one who is coming after me . . . ," said John, "will baptize you with the holy Spirit and fire" (Matt 3:11). Jesus baptizes in the Spirit: in giving us his Spirit, he makes us adopted children of the Father; he baptizes in fire, burning out the idols we adored; he burns out the sins we committed; he burns out the evil in us, our selfishness, our injustice, our pride. He delivers us from original sin.

What does a person become through baptism?

Through Christian baptism a new human being is born, a person who is saved. The baptized share in the paschal mystery of Christ: in humbly letting themselves be immersed in the water, they take part in the death of Christ; welcoming Christ's Spirit and receiving a new life, they rise out of the water and take part in the Lord's resurrection.

Having become an adopted child of the Father, the Christian enters the Church, taking on the dignity of a layperson, that is, becoming a member of the people of God, a member of the Body of Christ, a living rock of the Church, a temple of the Holy Spirit. The "old self," wounded by sin, lived alone; the "new self," delivered from sin, lives closely with his or her brothers and sisters in Christian community.

Do Christians realize their dignity?

"Christian, be aware of your dignity! Since you now share in the divine nature, do not degrade yourself by returning to the decadence of your past life. Call to mind the head to which you belong and the body of which you are a member. Remind yourself that you have been snatched from the powers of darkness to be transported into the light and the Kingdom of God" (St. Leo the Great).

God, the assembly, and the catechumen . . .

There are three responses in baptism: responses to the Word of God, to the word of the community, and to the word of the catechumen. The Word of God is the testimony of the Father who pardons us and adopts us, who saves us through his Son and gives us his Spirit. This Word marks us with an indelible seal. God does not take his Word back.

We are children of God forever. For this reason one cannot receive baptism a second time.

In turn, the community pledges its word by welcoming the newly baptized into the Church of God. Indeed, at the beginning of the sacrament's liturgy, the assembly proclaims in the catechumen's presence its profession of faith so that he or she may draw support from it.

Before receiving baptism, catechumens also pledge their word before God and the assembly: they renounce evil and Satan, and then join with the faith of those who have been their companions on the way by proclaiming their own profession of faith. These three responses show how baptism is the sacrament of faith and of faithfulness.

The main action of baptism involves three essential elements: the immersion of the catechumen into the water (or the pouring of the water over the head); the word of the minister of the sacrament:

"N., I baptize you
in the name of the Father
and of the Son
and of the Holy Spirit"

and finally the faith of the catechumen who accepts this word and the faith of the community (expressed especially by the parents who present their child for baptism).

Baptism is called the "bath of regeneration" because the immersion into water gives us a share in the death of Christ, and coming out of the water gives us a share in his resurrection. Water purifies and symbolizes life. It draws its meaning only from the Word that attests to the baptism and which the believing heart accepts. Baptism is also called, and rightly so, the sacrament of faith. It is the "passover" of the Christian; it is why the Church prefers to celebrate the baptism of adults at the Easter Vigil.

There are three rites that are essential to baptism: (1) The anointing with sacred chrism (perfumed oil blessed by the bishop), which anticipates the rite of confirmation that will be performed by the bishop. Historically, he was the one who gave the three sacraments of initiation to the catechumen in the course of the same celebration. (2) The vesting with the white garment symbolizes the gift of new life in the Lord for, says St. Paul, "You . . . have clothed yourselves with Christ" (Gal 3:27). This garment is white, like

What does the principal rite of baptism signify?

And the complementary rites?

the one worn by the transfigured Christ (Luke 9:29). (3) The third rite is the giving of the candle, lighted from the paschal candle, since the Lord gives light: "Now you are light in the Lord" (Eph 5:8). This is why baptism is called "illumination." The one who receives it ought to walk in the light of Christ and let it shine forth. Each year at the Easter Vigil we hold a lighted candle to remind ourselves that we live in this light and that we await Christ with vigilance "until he returns."

The minister of baptism is a bishop, a priest, or a deacon. In the event that someone is in danger of death, any person may baptize if it is sincerely performed and done according to the Church's intention.

Who can baptize?

The godfather and godmother are the community's witnesses. They must themselves be earnest Christians and be baptized and confirmed. Merely because they are relatives or friends is not sufficient reason for choosing them. Along with the parents, they are called upon to uphold the faith of the baptized throughout his or her new life by their example and counsel.

The godfather and the godmother

Preparation for an adult baptism takes place over an extended period called the "catechumenate." One uses as much time as needed so that the catechumen's request to be baptized might mature and that his or her desire be enlightened by the catechesis (teaching) given by the Christian community. This catechesis is accompanied by celebrations that mark the steps of an ever more intense preparation. These celebrations normally take place at the start of Lent and during the community's penitential liturgies, so that it is clear that conversion in Christ, dead and risen, is experienced together.

The baptism of adults

For the baptism of infants the Church desires an adequate preparation by the parents, so that they might better realize that the same grace of believing that was granted to them is also given so that they might educate their child in the faith. The faith that slumbers in a child's consciousness is quickened when his or her heart and intelligence awake. No catechesis can replace the one that goes with the first gesture of a child learning to make the sign of the cross or the one that teaches the child to talk with the Father from the time he babbles his first words to his parents. To have a child baptized is to promise to accompany that child in the life of faith. Thus the Church does not allow a child to be baptized against the will of the father and mother.

The baptism of infants: to what do parents commit themselves?

Certain parishes offer parents a veritable neocatechumenate, that is, a more or less lengthy period during which they learn to rediscover their own faith, renew their bonds with the community of believers, and receive help for the religious education of their children.

An infant born of Christian parents is born into a Christian community. What prevents him or her from being welcomed into the Church community? The Church is not reserved for adults alone, as if God had not summoned infants. When the disciples rebuked the people who brought their babies to Jesus so that he might touch them, he said, "Let the children come to me and do not prevent them; for the kingdom of God belongs to such as these . . . whoever does not accept the kingdom of God like a child will not enter it" (Luke 18:15-17).

What meaning is there in baptizing a newborn?

The baptism of small children manifests the gratuity of this gift of God. The responsibility of the community, particularly of the parents, is great, because the divine life the infants have received will not be able to mature without the witness and support of the people around them.

94

Confirmation

If baptism places the accent mainly on the remission of sin and on filial adoption, confirmation manifests above all the gift of the Spirit and the integration of the baptized into the missionary Church.

Asking to be confirmed in the faith of one's baptism . . .

To ask to be confirmed is an act of courage, for the Spirit leads and breathes where it will. It is necessary to announce the Lord and come out of the shadows to shine like a light that "gives light to all in the house," said the Lord. "You are the light of the world. A city set on a mountain cannot be hidden" (Matt 5:15, 14).

At baptism, the Christian receives the Holy Spirit who is at the origin of his or her new life. Yet there is a progression in the manifestation of God and in the communication of his Spirit.

Didn't we already receive the Holy Spirit in baptism?

Jesus is born of the Spirit. From the first instant of his life, he lived under its influence; yet, at the threshold of his public life, the Holy Spirit descended upon him to authenticate his mission.

The Church was born of the Spirit that Jesus communicated to it by his death and resurrection to make of it a new people. From the eve of Passover, the Church was filled with the Spirit (John 20:22). Yet on Pentecost morning, the Spirit quickened it with courage and missionary dynamism to carry the Church's testimony of faith throughout the world for all time.

In this manner, one can say that if the Lord's pasch was in some way the baptism of the Church, then Pentecost was its confirmation. The pasch of a Christian is his or her baptism, and confirmation renews in each of them, through the bishop's ministry, the gift of Pentecost.

The Acts of the Apostles relate to us that the Holy Spirit given to the Church of Jerusalem was imparted by the apostles to the baptized of Samaria:

When the apostles prayed and laid on hands . . .

"Now when the apostles in Jerusalem heard that Samaria had accepted the word of God, they sent them Peter and John, who went down and prayed for them, that they might receive the holy Spirit, for it had not yet fallen upon any of them; they had only been baptized in the name of the Lord Jesus. Then they laid hands on them and they received the holy Spirit" (Acts 8:14-17).

This testimony is important for understanding the nature of the sacrament of confirmation. The prayer of invocation for the coming of the Spirit (the prayer called the "epiclesis") and the gift of the Spirit through the laying on of hands by the bishop together shed light on the connection of this sacrament with Pentecost and the apostles.

How is confirmation to be understood within a Christian's progress?

During the first centuries of the Church, confirmation immediately followed baptism; it confirmed the inclusion of the Christian into the ecclesial community, and it prepared him or her for the Eucharist: the three sacraments' order of celebration remains the same as that of the sacramental initiation of an adult, and in the tradition of the Eastern Church as well. Throughout history and in different regions, this order had its variations. In the West, the times for conferring baptism, given by a priest, and confirmation, reserved to the bishop (or to a priest specially delegated by him), gradually diverged, and for practical reasons. They are no less tied together in their meaning. This is why at the beginning of the confirmation celebration the bishop invites the confirmands to renew their baptismal promises. The Liturgy of the Eucharist, during which confirmation is celebrated, underscores the unity of the three sacraments of initiation.

Confirmed in the people of God

The confirmands are prepared to renew their baptismal promises through a catechesis given by the community. During this preparatory period, in groups and with catechists, they learn to live in the Church. At their "profession of faith," they accept on their own the faith of the Church in which they have been baptized and which their parents and the community have handed on to them. They are once again assisted by sponsors who, as far as possible, are the same sponsors they had at baptism. They are surrounded by the whole community of believers, called together for this eminently ecclesial event.

The laying on of hands is a gesture rich with meaning. It variously signifies taking possession, investiture, and blessing. The bishop, along with the assisting priests, lays hands on all of the confirmands: this collective gesture emphasizes the unity of the priests and the bishop in the ministry that has consecrated them to the service of the Spirit. The bishop, by himself, says the prayer of invocation, asking that the Spirit who rested upon Jesus might be given in fullness to the confirmands: the spirit of wisdom and understand-

96

ing; the spirit of counsel and fortitude; the spirit of knowledge and piety, and the spirit of adoration.

This first imposition of hands upon all the confirmands is
followed by the imposition of the bishop's hands on each
confirmand at the moment when the bishop anoints his or
her forehead with sacred chrism while pronouncing these
words:

*What does the essential rite of
confirmation mean?*

*"N., be sealed
with the Gift of the Holy Spirit."*

The anointing is the essential gesture that unites the baptized to Christ, since the words "Christ" and "Christian"
signify "anointed." For the people of Israel, the action of
anointing someone was a consecration that indicated the
mission of prophet, king, or priest, through which the consecrated one received the Spirit of the Lord. Since oil is a
somewhat elusive substance, yet is penetrating and fortify-
ing, the oil symbolizes the Spirit. The sacred chrism is perfumed oil consecrated by the bishop. Its pleasant fragrance,
which each in turn is called upon to disseminate, is the joy
of living in the Spirit of the Lord. With this holy oil the bishop
signs each of the confirmed with a cross.

97

Through the anointing and the accompanying words, the baptized receives an indelible mark or "character," the "seal" of the Spirit: ". . . the holy Spirit of God with which you were sealed . . ." (Eph 4:30), says St. Paul. Indeed, confirmation seals the baptismal covenant.

We are marked by the faithfulness of God!

Like baptism and the sacrament of orders, confirmation is a rite of consecration that confers Christ's mission. To accomplish that mission God presents a gift of a permanent power, since he does not call a person to his service only to abandon him right away. That is why the Church says that these sacraments leave an indelible character. They can be received only once.

God is faithful, and it was he who called you to fellowship with his Son (1 Cor 1:9).

If we are unfaithful he will still remain faithful, for he cannot deny himself (2 Tim 2:13).

One day when Jesus went to the Nazareth synagogue, he read the text that was handed to him. In the prophecy of Isaiah, he acknowledged and announced his mission, which since that time is also ours:

"The spirit of the Lord is upon me,
because he has anointed me to bring glad tidings to the
    poor.
He has sent me to proclaim liberty to captives and
recovery of sight to the blind,
to let the oppressed go free, and
to proclaim a year acceptable to the Lord" (Luke 4:18-19).

The confirmed person is from then on a full-fledged member of the people of God, a "priestly people," a "community of priests." This priesthood is common to all the baptized. Its root lies in baptism and confirmation; it is expressed in those who receive the sacraments, who give witness by holy lives and effective charity. Indeed, if we are members of a priestly people, the laity—namely, the members of this people—ought to take an active part in the mission of the whole Church. This is one of the characteristics of the apostolate of laypeople in the world.

Is there a certain age for receiving the sacrament of confirmation?

The Catholic Church wants the sacrament of confirmation to be conferred at "the age of reason," just as for the reception of Eucharistic communion. This means that youngsters, now capable of interiorizing their love to the point of be-

98

ing able to offer it, can begin the catechesis that prepares them for confirmation. When renewing their baptismal promises, they will be able to discern the evil that they renounce and to confess their faith in God whom they love. Whenever this age of reason arrives, the baptized are ready to receive this sacrament and can request it. In our country, confirmation is generally given to young people between the ages of fourteen and seventeen. Parents and the parish community ought to help them fulfill their mission as confirmed Christians. This witness of young people revitalizes the faith of parents and the faith of the whole community.

Celebrating the Lord's Passover: the Eucharist

"You are my God, and I give thanks to you" (Ps 118:28).

Asking to be confirmed is an act of being open to the Spirit. Celebrating the Lord for the good that he does by giving us salvation is an act of gratitude. Celebrating the Eucharist means giving thanks, saying "thank you!"

An ungrateful heart gives no importance to what it has received. Refusing to acknowledge what may be given, it scorns the giver. A grateful heart rejoices in what it receives and acknowledges the giver. While thanking the Father for creation, we thank him further for his Son, who brings us from sin into grace, from death into resurrection.

The greatest of the sacraments

By this thanksgiving, we celebrate the mystery of faith, namely, the work of God. The Eucharist is the source and summit of all the other sacraments. Indeed, the others provide us with the good effects of salvation, but the Eucharist gives us the Lord himself, the source of our salvation. Through it Christ makes himself present to his Church and gives himself to us as nourishment.

What an honor it is to invite someone or be invited to a meal!

Jesus instituted the Eucharist during a meal. Many times he shared meals with his disciples, but also with others: at Cana, at Bethany, at the homes of notable Pharisees, or at those of equally well-known tax collectors, such as Matthew and Zacchaeus—in good company and some that were not so good! He came for sinners and to gather all the scattered children of God. The meal is the place to be elbow to el-

bow with one's brothers and sisters, where talk is shared, and where everyone is served from the same plate and drinks from the same cup. At the Eucharist, we are invited to the Lord's table, "the sinners' table."

One of the parables that Jesus tells about the end of times depicts a wedding banquet (Matt 22:1-14). The meal is a sign of salvation and of communion between God and humanity.

The Last Supper has a special character. Jesus celebrates the Passover with his disciples. He has so eagerly desired

"I have eagerly desired to eat this Passover with you" (Luke 22:15).

Last Supper. Fresco, School of Pietro Lorenzetti (1305–1348). Assisi.

it! This Holy Thursday meal anticipates the offering of his death for love of us and of "the multitude." Jesus reunites the Twelve and, beyond them, the Church. Even today he greatly desires to eat this Passover with us. The Eucharist is the promise, already realized as a seed from which we shall harvest the messianic meal at the end of time.

Celebrating the Passover in Jesus' time meant to eat the paschal lamb in memory of the escape from Egypt. Each family would choose a lamb without blemish and slaugh-

A meal different from others

ter it without breaking its bones. The blood of the lamb was seen as having two meanings. Before the flight from Egypt, it preserved from death the Hebrews who had marked the doorways of their houses with it. To ratify the covenant of Sinai, Moses sprinkled his people with the blood of sacrifice, the blood of the Covenant.

What does Christ's Passover mean for us?

When a loved one dies, it takes years to understand the loss. Meditating on Jesus' death, the beloved disciple John reminds us that not one of his bones was broken. By this he meant that Jesus was *the* paschal lamb. The other evangelists who describe the last paschal meal of Jesus do not speak of the lamb, since the Lamb is Christ. His blood is "the blood of the *new* covenant" concluded between God and *all* humanity.

Pasch means "passage": The pasch of the Jews celebrated the flight from Egypt; the Christian pasch celebrates the "passage of Christ" from this world to his Father (John 13:1). By opening this path, Jesus opened it for all humanity.

"Do this in memory of me," says Jesus. It is no longer a matter of calling to mind the deliverance from Egypt, but rather a deliverance from sin. The memorial of the death and resurrection of Jesus embraces the past, the present, and the future. Ever since the Lord's victory over sin and death, the Kingdom of God is here in our midst.

"If only you recognized God's gift!" (John 4:10).

The words of institution for the sacrament of the Eucharist: "This is my Body, given up for you . . . This is the cup of my Blood poured out for you" are the most important words that Jesus uttered on Holy Thursday. To share in the bread and the cup is to enter into personal communion with Christ who gives *himself* to us. Jesus entrusted these words to the Twelve and, through them, to the entire Church. They mean, "I am there for you." After twenty centuries the Church lives by these words and this presence; whether in peace or under persecution, injustice, or scorn, the Church will eat this bread and drink this cup until the end of time, when the Lord himself will come.

The words of Jesus are inseparable from the action that they describe: he took bread, gave thanks, and *"broke* it." This breaking is more than a practical necessity. It is the sign of the gift that Jesus made of himself in his passion: he was broken by suffering because of our offenses. The prophet Isaiah had foretold it (Isa 53:4-5). After the resurrection, when Jesus appeared to the disciples on the way to Em-

102

maus, it was at the breaking of the bread in the evening
that they recognized him (Luke 24:13-35). The Book of Acts
teaches us that the disciples were faithful to the "breaking
of the bread." This is what the Eucharist was called in the
Church's early times.

Faithful to the Lord's command "Do this in memory of me,"
Christians gather on the first day of the week to celebrate
the Lord's Supper. Participation in the Eucharist of Saturday evening or Sunday is the most important expression of
faith and of communion with Christ dead and risen. The
Eucharist gathers believers into community: it creates the
Church. This is why the Church asks all the faithful to be
present. Not to participate in the Lord's Supper is to have
a certain disdain for the Church.

Are we faithful?

The different stages in the Liturgy of the Eucharist reveal
its meaning: the introductory rites, the proclamation of the
Word of God, the Lord's Supper, the dismissal of the assembly. Each Eucharist recalls the Easter feast, a sign of communion, a foretaste of the heavenly liturgy, a share in eternal
life: it shows what the world will be when "God [will] be
all in all" (1 Cor 15:28).

*How do we find our way through
the course of the celebration?*

Introductory Rite

The celebration begins with the sign of the cross, since it
is in the name of the Father, the Son, and the Holy Spirit
that we are assembled and the liturgy unfolds. What would
the celebration be if God were not in the midst of the assembly and did not preside over it! For this reason the
bishop or the priest greets the assembly by saying, *"The
Lord be with you."*

The Church is a people of pardoned sinners. They acknowledge this by confessing God's mercy: together, they implore, *"Lord, have mercy!"*

Following the words of pardon, the assembly raises its hymn
of praise: *"Glory to God in the highest . . ."* The celebrant
invites the community to pray in silence, then gathers ("col-
lects") the prayer of all into one prayer: may the Lord increase our faith, hope, and love; may he open our
understanding and our hearts to receive the message of this
day.

*The Church: an assembly
convoked by God*

103

Proclamation of the Word

In the Liturgy of the Word, it is the Lord who speaks. The first reading, normally taken from the Old Testament, prefigures and announces the mystery of Christ and his Church. The second reading, from the Acts of the Apostles, the letters of the apostles, or from the Book of Revelation, makes the apostolic preaching reverberate in our ears. The third reading is the Gospel, the Good News of Jesus Christ. The Sunday readings are divided into three years (A, B, C), in the course of which we read, above all, the Gospels of Matthew, Mark, and Luke, while the Gospel of John is read each year during the high seasons of Christmas, Lent, and the Sundays of Eastertide.

"To listen [to him] like a disciple, the Lord Yahweh has opened my ear" (Isa 50:4, JB).

In the homily, or exhortation to the assembly, the priest or deacon makes relevant for us Christians the Word that has just been proclaimed. After that, we rise and together profess one faith in proclaiming the Creed of the Church.

The Liturgy of the Word is concluded by the prayer of the faithful, through which we invoke the Father on behalf of the Church, the world, and ourselves. We thus prepare ourselves to enter into the great thanksgiving with an open heart.

The Lord's Supper

With what attitude do we make ready the table of the Kingdom?

Listening to the Word flows into the Liturgy of the Eucharist, properly speaking, or the great thanksgiving. At this point we move from the table of the Word to the table of the Bread. The "offerings," bread and wine, are brought up to the priest, who accepts them and offers them to the Father. The faithful join with this offering by making a gift of themselves in the offering of bread and wine. At this point, in an action of brotherly sharing and in accordance with the tradition that goes back to apostolic times (Acts 2:42-45), the faithful assembled for the "breaking of the bread" give of their material wealth for the needs of the poor and of the community.

A marvelous exchange between God and humans?

The rite of preparation is concluded by the prayer over the gifts. The celebrant asks the Lord to accept our gifts, to change them into the gift of eternal life, and to make living offerings of us, pleasing to the Lord. This prayer evokes the wondrous exchange between God and humanity and makes us sharers in the divine nature.

Now the great Eucharistic Prayer begins. Again the celebrant greets and gathers the participants with these words: *"The Lord be with you!"* The Lord who has spoken to his people during the Liturgy of the Word is about to make himself present under the sign of bread and wine. Jesus is the priest who assembles us, since he is the one who gives his life. He is also the perfect offering, because he pleases the Father in everything.

From praise to adoration

The preface is the thanksgiving that rises to the Father who has created us and recreated us in his Son, Jesus Christ our Lord. The assembly joins in with it at the hymn of adoration: *"Holy, holy, holy Lord!"*

The priest extends his hands over the bread and wine while praying to the Father that he might send his Spirit. This prayer is called the "epiclesis" or invocation: *"Let your Spirit come upon these gifts to make them holy, so that they may become for us the body and blood of our Lord, Jesus Christ"* (Eucharistic Prayer II).

Invocation over the offerings

The words of institution are recited in the Eucharistic Prayer:

Consecration: the Lord is really present.

"Before he was given up to death,
a death he freely accepted,
he took bread and gave you thanks.
He broke the bread,
gave it to his disciples, and said:
Take this, all of you, and eat it:
this is my body which will be given up for you.
When supper was ended, he took the cup.
Again he gave you thanks and praise,
gave the cup to his disciples, and said:
Take this, all of you, and drink from it:
this is the cup of my blood,
the blood of the new and everlasting covenant.
It will be shed for you and for all
so that sins may be forgiven.
Do this in memory of me."

The Lord's work of salvation is the great mystery of faith that we proclaim in thanksgiving. The Eucharistic memorial actualizes and sacramentally makes present the universal sacrifice of Christ on the cross. Yet the Lord's death is inseparable from his resurrection and his return to the Father, together with whom he is eternally living. The Eucharist is

We do this in memory not of someone absent but of him who lives.

the memorial (*anamnesis*) of the whole paschal mystery in which we share. The entire assembly proclaims it:

"Dying you destroyed our death,
Rising you restored our life.
Lord Jesus, come in glory."

The celebrant continues the prayer and offers with the whole Church the Body and Blood of Christ to the Father.

May the Spirit come upon the assembly!

At the core of the Eucharistic mystery, the priest invokes the Father that he might send his Holy Spirit upon the assembly: that they might become, through Christ's sacrifice, one body and one living offering to the glory of the Father (second epiclesis).

Remember, Lord, the Church of the living and of the dead.

The prayers of intercession follow: for the pope, the bishops, and the entire people of God; for the dead, for those assembled, and the living. We ask the Virgin and the saints and the great community of the Church in heaven and on earth to intercede for us before the Father.

The Eucharistic Prayer culminates in a brief and profound "Eucharist," or prayer of thanks and praise, addressed to the Holy Trinity. The entire assembly responds with a resounding *"Amen."*

After this acclamation (doxology) the communion liturgy begins. The communal recitation or singing of the "Our Father" leads into the sign of peace expressing the fellowship of love and preparing the faithful to communicate with Christ.

The breaking of bread, through which the priest repeats Jesus' action, is the sign by which the disciples on the road to Emmaus recognized the Lord.

What are the requirements for receiving the Lord's Body?

To communicate with Christ means to recognize in him "the Lamb of God who takes away the sin of the world." It is an act of faith of immense seriousness. St. Paul expresses himself on the matter in very strong terms:

"Therefore whoever eats the bread or drinks the cup of the Lord unworthily will have to answer for the body and blood of the Lord. A person should examine himself first, and so eat the bread and drink the cup. For anyone who eats and drinks without discerning the body, eats and drinks judgment on himself" (1 Cor 11:27-29).

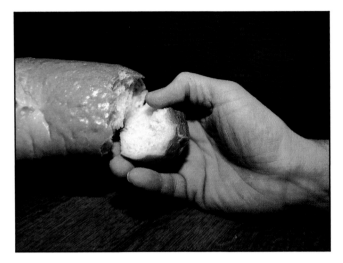

To eat the bread and to drink the cup of the Lord unworthily is to commit an offense against the grace of our baptism, through which we became children of God and faithful to the Lord. We communicate unworthily when we do so with indifference or without being reconciled, in the case of grave sin, through the sacrament of reconciliation.

It is important to prepare children well, both within the family and in the Christian community, to receive the Body of the Lord with faith. It is not enough for them to be prepared just once and for all; rather, they should see that their parents and the community always prepare with a continuing effort to conform to the gospel.

After taking part in Jesus' paschal mystery, we die and we rise with the Lord.

This nourishment gives life beyond death:

"Whoever eats my flesh
and drinks my blood
has eternal life . . .
the one who feeds on me
will have life because of me" (John 6:54, 57).

In the course of the Eucharist we have constantly called upon God's forgiveness: *"Lord, have mercy," "I confess to God," "May almighty God have mercy on us," "Forgive us our trespasses," "Lord . . . only say the word and I shall be healed."* Communion with the Body of Christ remits our sins and unites us to him. For "whoever is joined to the Lord becomes one spirit with him" (1 Cor 6:17).

The fruits of this sacrament?
A superabundant life

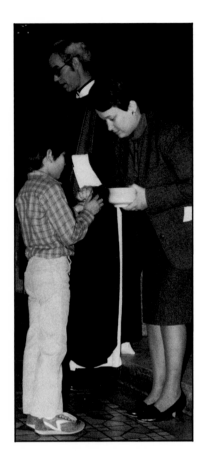

The whole Church is missionary.

The Eucharist, the gift of Christ dead and risen, is the source of all powers of healing. The Church affirms that the Lord's Body does in fact heal the entire person. The other sacraments of healing, such as baptism, reconciliation, and anointing of the sick, draw from this living source.

Each communion with the Body of Christ is also a communion with our brothers and sisters. The broken and shared bread confirms our unity in love. The Eucharist is the "sign of unity" and the "bond of love"; it is Jesus Christ, bread broken for a new world, sacrament of sharing and of Christian life in its fullness.

In giving communion St. Augustine would say to each one, "Become what you are receiving: the Body of Christ." To this cogent invitation we answer with faith, "Amen." The Eucharist has given strength and joy to the hearts of the poor. If lived in depth, it will bring forth its fruits in daily existence. As St. Paul said, in a moment of jubilation: "Yet I live, no longer I, but Christ lives in me!" (Gal 2:20).

When we are tempted to say, "The Eucharist is so far removed from our lives," should we not, on the contrary, recognize that our lives are too far removed from the Eucharist?

Dismissal of the Assembly

The celebration is concluded by the benediction and by the assembly being sent forth, as on a mission. This is where the word "Mass" comes from, meaning "sending":

"Go, in the peace of Christ!"

108

Funeral Celebration

The death of a brother or sister is an event that touches not only the family of the deceased but also the community. In this event we enounter God the Father, Son, and Holy Spirit.

The funeral rite is not a sacrament. The deceased has already left us, and God reveals himself to him or her no longer through signs but now face to face. This is why the community gathers on the death of one of its own. In celebrating a funeral, it celebrates Christ's passover. It prays that the dead pass with Christ from death to life, that they be purified in their souls and join with all the saints in heaven, awaiting the resurrection of the dead and the blissful expectation of the coming of Christ. We assert that we remain in communion with the dead, thanks to Christ with whom we communicate.

On the occasion of a funeral, we grasp more clearly how each sacrament, particularly the Eucharist, reveals to us the Kingdom and gives us a share now in the life of the world to come. In surrounding the body of the deceased with respect for having been the temple of the Holy Spirit, we believe that the Spirit which raised up Jesus will also raise up our dead.

The funeral liturgy begins at the home of the deceased or, more often, the funeral home, and follows with the Eucharistic thanksgiving and the rites and prayers of the final farewell. It concludes with the rite of ''interment,'' that is, burial in the ground as with Christ's body (or the prayer before cremation). All these actions proclaim the Christian community's faith in the resurrection.

Dead and living, we stay united in the Body of Christ.

Temple of the Holy Spirit

Reconciliation with God

The sacrament of reconciliation is the sign that we are at peace with God and the community. It lifts up the sinner and restores a sense of worthiness to his or her innermost being. It is a source of joy and renewal for the Church.

The parables of mercy, such as those about the prodigal son and the lost sheep, bring out God's joy at the conversion of a sinner and the attention he gives to such a person: " 'Rejoice with me because I have found my lost sheep.' I tell you, in just the same way there will be more joy in heaven over one sinner who repents than over ninety-nine righteous people who have no need of repentance" (Luke 15:6-7). And Jesus insists, ". . . I tell you, there will be rejoicing among the angels of God over one sinner who repents" (Luke 15:10).

On the evening of Holy Thursday, Jesus anticipated the gift of his life by having his disciples drink from the cup: "Take this, all of you, and drink from it: this is the cup of my blood, the blood of the new and everlasting covenant (reconciliation). It will be shed for you and for all men so that sins may be forgiven." On the cross, Jesus forgave his executioners as he died and, in the offering of his Son to the Father, God reconciles the world with himself (2 Cor 5:19).

The remission of sins is a gift from Jesus to sinners and to the world, in the Church.

The Lord's cross is the icon of our reconciliation. "But if anyone does sin, we have an Advocate with the Father, Jesus Christ the righteous one. He is expiation for our sins, and not for our sins only but for those of the whole world (1 John 2:1-2).

The power of remitting sins belongs to God alone. On the evening of Easter, when the Risen Jesus appeared to his apostles, he bestowed his Spirit upon them so that they might pardon sins in his name. The first mission they were given was to pardon, and Jesus conferred the power on them by saying,

Jesus confers upon the apostles the power of forgiving.

"As the Father has sent me,
so I send you. . . .
Receive the holy Spirit.
Whose sins you forgive are forgiven them,
and whose sins you retain are retained" (John 20:21-23).

Today, this ministry of reconciliation is entrusted to bishops and, through them, to priests. Indeed, at ordination, the

Church confers upon them the power about which Jesus spoke: "Whatever you bind on earth shall be bound in heaven, and whatever you loose on earth shall be loosed in heaven" (Matt 18:18).

"For the love of Christ impels us . . . be reconciled to God" (2 Cor 5:14, 20).

Baptism makes us members of the Body of Christ, brothers and sisters for each other. Through the Eucharist we communicate with the Lord and with our sisters and brothers. Yet who has not experienced how the bonds of this unity are strained as a consequence of our negligence and failures? Every sin is a wound, a rupture of the bonds that unite us: "something" where "nothing is right" between God and us, between others and us. The consequences of sin are considerable. They affect more than just our personal life. Indeed, to act against God is to contribute to the disorder that sin introduces and perpetuates in the Church and in the world. Sin has cosmic repercussions. The cross of Christ reveals this to us.

Why confess to a priest?

All the baptized form one body in Christ. Just as the holiness of one mysteriously benefits all the others, in the same way the sins of one harm the whole body. Likewise, in the sacrament, the priest represents not only Christ, through whom God reconciles us to himself; he also represents the Christian community that we have wounded; he restores us to its communion. Indeed, what more serious thing could befall a member than to be cut off from the body to which it belongs? This is why the sacrament of reconciliation heals not only the sinner but also the Church, for "if one [member] suffers, all the [members] suffer with it; if one [member] is honored, all the [members] share its joy. Now you are Christ's body, and individually [members] of it" (1 Cor 12:26-27). Penitents who open their hearts to a priest know that they are talking with another sinner, also pardoned by Christ; he accepts them as a brother or sister but also as the representative of Christ, friend of sinners.

Conversion in the Church

Nowadays two forms of celebrating forgiveness are generally used: the individual reconciliation of a penitent, which can be conducted at any time, and the communal celebration of reconciliation with individual confessions and absolutions; these take place mainly at special times for conversion and penance, such as Lent or Advent or the preparation for some major feast.

The communal celebrations highlight the ecclesial dimension of the sacrament. They are made up of four stages:

1) Responding to the call of Christ and the Church, the sinners assemble and greet one another in the faith. The community, gathered around its pastor, asks God to grant them true conversion.

2) Together, the penitents listen to God's Word, examine their lives in relation to him, and pray for one another.

3) Those who desire the sacrament confess their sins individually to a priest and receive personal absolution.

4) The assembly gives thanks to God for the gift of his mercy and receives God's blessing through the ministry of the celebrant. All are then sent forth to live by, and to carry to the world, the Good News of pardon and reconciliation.

Sin, fault, guilt, bitterness, remorse and disappointment, contrition or indifference? A host of feelings, sometimes contradictory, stir our consciences. We have an acute sense of evil spread through the world; we feel ourselves capable of everything and responsible for nothing. It is possible for our conscience to delude itself or, contrarily, to harden. "If we say, 'We are without sin,' we deceive ourselves and the truth is not in us" (1 John 1:8). On questions concerning formation of conscience, an authentic sense of sin, and contrition, we invite the reader to turn to pp. 158–164, part of "Living the Gospel."

"For I acknowledge my offense!" (Ps 51:5).

The desire to repent, aroused by the Spirit, moves sinners to confess. This grace that inspires sinners to regret having offended God and harmed their brothers and sisters does not turn them inward; rather, it furthers their return with their entire being toward the Father who waits for them. Repenting is so important for entering into this reconciliation that the word "penance" for a long time was sufficient to identify the sacrament: sins are not remitted except for those who regret them and resolutely decide to struggle in order to convert themselves. Accordingly, after the confession of sins, the rite requires the priest to ask the penitent to pray and to perform some action that conforms to the meaning of love, truth, and justice: "Love covers a multitude of sins" (1 Pet 4:8). The encounter between the penitent and the priest is not a plain conversation. It is a trusting dialogue that is wreathed in prayer from beginning to end. They welcome each other through a shared sign of the cross, and the priest begins by blessing the penitent. The latter then makes his or her "confession."

Be a penitent?

To confess means both to acknowledge God's love and mercy and to avow one's sins: "In behaving this way and that—in thought, word, and deed, or by omission—I have sinned." It is not so much a question of enumerating one's sins as of humbly recognizing them and allowing the priest to determine their seriousness so that he might counsel the penitent. The penitent's self-accusation is thus both beneficial and liberating.

It is in Christ's name that the priest receives penitents, reveals the Father's mercy to them, and listens to the secrets of their consciences. Because of this ministry, he is bound never to reveal these sacramental secrets. After hearing a confession, the priest sometimes counsels the penitent and proposes an act of penance to make satisfaction for his or her sins. Then he prays with the penitent to receive forgiveness (*Act of Contrition*, p. 82).

To *absolve* means "to unbind," to deliver the penitent from his or her ties to sin. Lazarus was likewise covered with bands of cloth that kept him captive in death. And so when

114

Jesus raised him to life again, he said, "Untie him and let him go" (John 11:44). Absolution is, by the grace of God, radical and total pardon of sin; it is resurrection into the divine life. It completely reestablishes the believer in his or her condition as a son or daughter of God and as an integral member of the community of the ransomed. The gesture of absolution—laying on of hands as a sign of the gift of the Spirit—is accompanied by the sacramental word that brings out the action of the Father, the Son, and the Holy Spirit through the Church's mediation:

"God the Father of mercies,
through the death and resurrection of his Son,
has reconciled the world to himself
and sent the Holy Spirit among us
for the forgiveness of sins;
through the ministry of the Church
may God give you pardon and peace,
And I absolve you from your sins
in the name of the Father, and of the Son, ✝ and of
  the Holy Spirit."

"A clean heart create for me, O God. Give me back the joy of your salvation" (Ps 51:12, 14).

Receiving God's pardon with faith and joy, the believer answers *"Amen,"* and the priest sends the penitent off in the peace and joy of Christ. The pardoned sinner experiences reconciliation with God, with him- or herself, with others, and with all of creation. The Spirit dwelling in them makes them witnesses of his pardon and leads them to make up for the evil they have done, to the extent that they can.

The renewal achieved through use of the sacrament of reconciliation touches first of all upon the interior life: for the root of all goodness (and of all evil) is found deep within one's heart. It is there that personal change is initiated in attitude, in mentality, in mode of life. Among the "works of penance," Scripture and tradition contain three main ones: sharing of goods, prayer, and fasting (Matt 6:1-18). Respectively, these three forms of conversion are in direct relation to others, to God, and to oneself. In a world where people live in conflict, yet desire liberty, justice, unity, and peace, the sacrament of reconciliation renews society as well. The demands of total conversion to God and the grace of forgiveness can be a firm basis on which to build the relationships of justice and brotherhood that the world longs for.

Is confession an isolated and specific act?

115

Is confession required?

The Church requires the faithful to confess their serious faults at least once a year. It also demands that Christians be converted from their serious sins and receive the sacrament of reconciliation before receiving the other sacraments.

How can one sit at the table of unity and commune with the Body and Blood of Christ if one has seriously turned away from the Father or if one has gravely harmed one's neighbor?

Even without these trespasses, it is good to approach God's merciful face regularly in this sacrament. If we often confess the same sins, they point out to us our weaknesses and are further reason for resorting frequently to the healing that the Lord gives. Forgiveness is one of the most characteristic signs of Christian life: forgive "seventy times seven times" (Matt 18:22), that is, without limit. How can human beings forgive each other mutually if not by learning how ready God is to forgive?

Is it necessary to receive the sacrament regularly?

Every contrite and pardoned sinner knows from experience that deep-rooted attitudes and behavior that are contrary to God's will remain in his or her life. As the Savior's humble minister and as a mother, the Church upholds the baptized in their weakness and in their struggle against the "effects of sin" and in their efforts to repair the damage caused by their offenses.

How are indulgences to be understood?

Christ is our "justice" and he is also our "indulgence." He is the one who remits deserved punishments. The Church brings converted sinners to share in this gift of Christ's indulgence when they show sincerely and generously, through acts of penance, devotion, and communal fellowship, that they want to live resolutely in the love of Christ and of others, in truth and in justice.

All the baptized, living or dead, belong to the communion of saints. They live in the holiness of Christ and, as sinners, find help in the charity of all the members of this Body who work for their conversion. This is a major type of ecclesial charity.

"With [the Lord] is plenteous redemption" (Ps 130:7).

By virtue of this immense wealth of the merits of Christ, the Church gives to all Christians the possibility of coming to the aid of their deceased brothers and sisters or as an aid to themselves regarding the remission of punishments that remain after absolution. This is why the Church generally recommends prayers and acts of penance and charity in order to take advantage of this treasury of pardon and reparation. Through this gift of indulgences, the Church wants to stimulate prayer, penance, and love in the faithful in order to have them share in the fullness of Christ within the communion of saints.

The Anointing of the Sick

Sickness is a trial that comes to everyone.

Sickness and suffering raise serious questions in our minds. A person not only *has* a sickness, he or she *is* sick. Sickness affects the body and the spirit as well, the entire person. Sometimes the sick person loses courage, becomes depressed, experiences anguish and doubt: "Have I deserved this trial? Will I recover from it? Does my life still have meaning? Is there anything (or Anyone) after death?"

It can also happen that relationships with other people are also affected: one feels dependent on others, visits become rare, and one seems to be excluded from social life.

"If one part [of the community] suffers, all the parts suffer with it (1 Cor 12:26).

The Christian community has always attached great importance to visiting and caring for the sick. Many laypeople, as well as many religious, have dedicated their whole lives to serving the sick with their medical and technical competence and their pastoral help. A great number of religious orders are dedicated entirely to this vocation.

In places of pilgrimage, in parishes, and in hospitals, the sacrament of the sick is celebrated in a communal manner, thus showing how much the whole community is concerned and shares the trials of its members.

Do you believe in the power of Christ against evil, and for life?

How could God have left us in sickness and distress unless he gave us an effective sign of his saving presence? The anointing of the sick allays suffering and calms anxieties. It does not replace medical care, but it consecrates, so to speak, the effort expended by physicians and nurses, and it also confers a Christian meaning of salvation upon the measures employed. These do not always succeed. A human being is fragile, and our earthly life is not without end. But "we have set our hope on the living God" (1 Tim 4:10).

Is sickness connected to sin?

God has not created evil, and he does not will suffering. Suffering came into the world through original sin. To struggle against sickness is to combat evil, of which it is the sign and consequence.

While physicians can heal many illnesses, only Jesus can entirely conquer sickness and sin. The sacrament of anointing is the sign of this grace that saves and heals.

According to the Gospels, to be healed is not only to recover health but even more to be freed from the powers

118

of evil so as to receive the Kingdom of God. Indeed, the Twelve that were sent by Jesus "went off, and preached repentance. They drove out many demons, and they anointed with oil many who were sick and cured them" (Mark 6:12-13).

After the resurrection, the disciples continued to witness to Jesus' compassion for the sick by healing many ill people (Acts 8:7). They therefore gave witness that the Risen One is the source of life. We read in the Epistle of St. James:

"Is anyone among you suffering? He should pray. Is anyone in good spirits? He should sing praise. Is anyone among

To heal . . . even at the root of evil.

Is one among you ill?

119

you sick? He should summon the presbyters of the church, and they should pray over him and anoint [him] with oil in the name of the Lord, and the prayer of faith will save the sick person, and the Lord will raise him up. If he has committed any sins, he will be forgiven'' (James 5:13-15).

This text shows how, from the beginning, the Church has understood Jesus' mandate to his disciples: ''Cure the sick'' (Matt 10:8).

The prayer of the early Christians and the anointing fore-tell the form that the sacrament gradually takes; the faith of the Church and of the believers join together to achieve the salvation of soul and body. The living Christ marks the injured human beings with his compassion; he saves them and lifts them up altogether: the deep peace resulting from the reconciliation of the sick person with God and with his or her illness improves each one's disposition for benefit-ing from the therapeutic efforts undertaken by the physician.

The sacrament of anointing renews trust in God, gives strength to combat temptation, and confirms the sacrament of reconciliation. Indeed, it remits the sins that the ill per-son was unable to confess *and* corrects the consequences of sin in him or her. Already anointed through the sacra-ment of confirmation at the springtime of their Christian lives in order to become adult and strong, the sick at this point receive additional grace to confront their trials in sickness.

Do you want to share in Christ's anointing?

Is this sacrament, once called "extreme unction," reserved for the dying? Primarily, it is intended for Christians affected by an illness that could lead to death. But it is not neces-sary to wait until the point of death in order to receive this sacrament. One may also request it when old age results in diminished strength or before an operation carrying se-rious risk.

Except in emergencies, the anointing of the sick is cele-brated in the context of a prayer liturgy that normally in-cludes one or more readings of the Word. It can also be celebrated within Mass, when circumstances allow.

"Be reconciled to God!"
(2 Cor 5:20).

The priest begins with a sprinkling of holy water, which recalls baptismal water. If the sick person wishes it, he or she immediately receives the sacrament of reconciliation. Otherwise, those present recite the *"I confess to almighty God."* There follows a scriptural reading and then a prayer.

It is good for the family, friends, and medical staff to take part in this celebration. Their familiar faces, serene prayer, and presence are the visible sign of the attention that God gives to the sick person, as well as of the solidarity of the Christian community with suffering men and women.

"I was . . . ill and you cared for me" (Matt 25:36).

The priest then silently lays hands on the sick person's head. Jesus performed this action many times (Mark 6:5; Matt 8:3; Luke 4:40), telling the disciples to do likewise (Mark 16:18).

"But come, lay your hand on her, and she will live" (Matt 9:18).

The imposition of hands is a gesture of intense prayer to

121

God that he might be with the sick person and that his Spirit might protect, encourage, and give him or her life.

"They . . . anointed with oil many who were sick . . ." (Mark 6:13).

Anointing with the oil of the sick (blessed by the bishop on Holy Thursday) also replicates an action of the apostles. Its meaning is made clear by the sacramental word of the priest to which the sick person responds with faith.

"N., through this holy anointing may the Lord in his love and mercy help you with the grace of the Holy Spirit.
Amen.
May the Lord who frees you from sin save you and raise you up.
Amen."

What does this sacrament ask a sick person to do?

A sick person can ask for the sacrament at the time of a visit by a priest or by a member of the group responsible for pastoral care of the sick, who will relay the request to a priest. It is good for the family, the physician, friends, or nurses to encourage this request. The sacrament will give the sick person the grace to struggle physically and spiritually in his or her suffering. As with the other sacraments, the anointing confers a mission upon the sick. It invites them to unite themselves freely to Christ's passion and death and

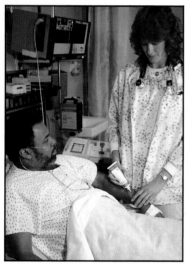

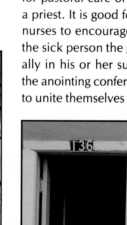

to carry their share for the good of the people of God (*Lumen Gentium*, 11).

The grace of the sacrament radiates through daily life: it furthers the community's action in taking charge of the sick and also the awareness of the role of the sick in the community. Are not many among them great people of prayer who intercede for us?

The last sacrament is not the anointing of the sick, but is holy communion when given as *viaticum,* which means "provisions for a journey." The Eucharist, the unsurpassed paschal sacrament, is the spiritual nourishment that prepares the believer to pass from this world to the Father.

The last sacrament?

Christian initiation is accomplished through baptism, confirmation, and the Eucharist. The preparation for the last journey is provided by the grace of reconciliation, anointing, and viaticum.

From baptism to viaticum

On the threshold of death, believers direct themselves toward the completion of their paschal journey begun on the day of their baptism. In receiving for the last time Christ's Body and Blood, they prepare to receive the mercy of God, which, throughout their lives, the sacraments never failed to give them.

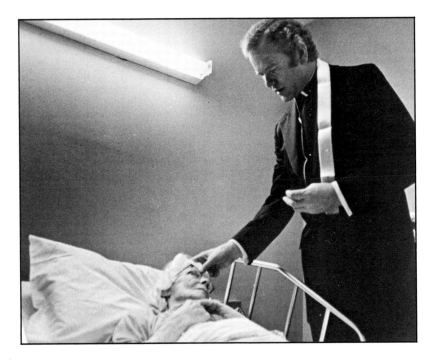

When Christians Marry

Work and leisure give nobility and pleasure to our existence; marriage brings to it a profound bond of life and love.

*Called by God to conjugal and
familial love . . .*

Founding a family requires the total gift of oneself. Christ
has elevated the bond between spouses to the dignity of
a sacrament. The couple draw from it strength and courage to help and love each other in good times and in bad;
they are also given a certain joy and openness to the pros-
pect of accepting children and raising them. Marriage consists essentially of the mutual commitment of the spouses.
It gives to them the same love that unites Christ to his
Church forever. Indeed, as St. Paul writes, the covenant between spouses is a sign of that union:

"Husbands, love your wives, even as Christ loved the
church and handed himself over to sanctify her. . . . This
is a great mystery, but I speak in reference to Christ and
the church" (Eph 5:25-26, 32).

In this beautiful and difficult undertaking, a man and a
woman desire to live their lives together. Acknowledging
their sins and moved by the Spirit of Christ given them in
baptism, they want to commit themselves to each other with
pure and open hearts. It is only natural, then, that they ask
for the grace of the sacrament of reconciliation in order to
share in the Eucharist on their wedding day.

Preparing oneself in the faith

A look at the marriage liturgy shows that it is not the priest
who marries the betrothed couple; they marry each other
through mutual consent: *They* give the sacrament to each
other in the presence of the priest, who gives to their commitment its ecclesial meaning, and in the presence of witnesses, who represent society.

*Who confers the sacrament of
marriage? And under what
conditions?*

In acting in the name of Christ and the Church, the spouses remain fully themselves. To celebrate their marriage, they must be free and aware of their promises. That is why the priest, who receives their promises in the name of the Church, questions them:

"N. and N., have you come here freely and without reservation to give yourselves to each other in marriage? Will you love and honor each other as man and wife for the rest of your lives? Will you accept children lovingly from God and bring them up according to the law of Christ and his Church?"

Being free, committing oneself for life to one person, and accepting responsibilities as spouses and parents—these are the conditions the Church sets forth for the couple to be truly joined in marriage.

The sacramental contract, an act of trust in God

Having entered the church as fiancés, they now leave it as husband and wife. This change is effected by their exchange of consent, the essential moment of the sacrament that begins their union of life and love. The sacramental character is manifested and assured by the presence of the Church, that is, normally by the priest who asks for their mutual consent in the presence of two witnesses. These attest to the public commitment of the spouses, and they sign the parish register along with the priest, after he has accepted their promises.

The priest says:

"Since it is your intention to enter into marriage, join your right hands, and declare your consent before God and his Church."

The couple hold hands and exchange their promises.

The bridegroom says:

"I, N., take you, N., to be my wife. I promise to be true to you in good times and in bad, in sickness and in health. I will love you and honor you all the days of my life."

The bride says:

"I, N., take you, N., to be my husband. I promise to be true to you in good times and in bad, in sickness and in health. I will love you and honor you all the days of my life."

126

This dialogue is simple and clear. The fiancés look forward to it and prepare themselves accordingly. Married people experience it anew and live by it. In this sacrament where the two become one flesh, it is Christ who speaks through each one. It is he who, through the mouth of each spouse, speaks of his love for the Church. When the bride speaks, Christ speaks; when the bridegroom answers, Christ answers. In doing this, neither he nor she is deprived of his or her being; the two speak freely, promise themselves to each other for life, and take up their responsibilities. Their word is a word of love, free and pure, one to another, yet at the same time a pure gift of God.

Through the exchange of promises, Christ seals the union of the spouses.

There are several formulas for exchanging promises, but all state the same truth. The priest says, in the name of the Church, that he accepts the commitment of the spouses as sealed. He extends his right hand over the couple and says,

Joined by God each day, until the last evening . . .

"*You have declared your consent before the Church.*
May the Lord in his goodness strengthen your consent
and fill you both with his blessings.
What God has joined, men must not divide."

These words echo the Gospel: "Therefore, what God has joined together, no human being must separate" (Matt 19:6). All the grandeur and beauty of the sacrament is contained in these words.

After giving thanks, the priest blesses the rings and the spouses give them to one another as a sign of their promise. "Promise"—a significant word, a precious symbol of love and fidelity!

The celebration can continue with a prayer of the spouses, preferably composed by themselves. In response, the priest and assembly pray for the new family or else continue into the Liturgy of the Eucharist.

*From marriage to the Eucharist . . .
throughout life!*

A wedding is most often celebrated during a Mass, between the Liturgy of the Word, which sheds light on it, and the Liturgy of the Eucharist, which gives it its paschal dimension. This relationship between the two sacraments is significant. Spouses who will share the same daily table look for grace and strength at the table of the Lord. Thus, after having given themselves to each other through their consent, they cannot deprive themselves of remembering it at the moment of consecration: "On the night he was betrayed, he took bread . . . and said, 'This is my body which will be given up for you.' " From this New Covenant, the gift of Christ, they draw their own covenant. That is why, for their entire lifetimes, they will participate in the Sunday Eucharist as a matter of respect.

After the wedding celebration the man and woman begin their common life. For them it will be a continual discovery, day after day, year after year. Marriage can be lived in loving joyfulness, yet it can also produce great disappointments. Human love is a calling that is lived through the experiences of joy and pain, conflict and forgiveness—even failure. We are in the image of God who is love, and that fills us with hope. Each day spouses are called upon to show Christ's attention to each other. They will be supported in their vocation by the Christian community, by families, and by those who have chosen celibacy for the sake of the Kingdom. Christians joyfully hope that love will overcome selfishness. The couple is called upon to have frequent recourse to prayer and to the sacrament of reconciliation.

Human sexuality is inclined toward the conjugal act. Just as language is word and silence, so sexuality is lived out by both engaging in intercourse and in abstaining. Each mode of sexuality is a form of love and respect for the other person. Thus the conjugal act, through which the spouses consummate their marriage, has definitive meaning. "A marriage, once contracted and consummated, cannot be dissolved by any human power nor by any cause, except death" (Code of Canon Law, can. 1141). The spouses belong exclusively to one another and the mutual gift of their sexuality is likewise exclusive, like the union of Christ and the Church. In the same way that the Church is one and its union with the Lord is unique, so is the conjugal tie between baptized spouses unique and unalterable; neither divorce nor adultery can dissolve it (Mark 10:6-9).

Marital sex always calls for serious consideration that should be neither burdensome nor trifling. In speaking about married people, St. Paul says, ". . . if they cannot exercise self-control they should marry, for it is better to marry than to be on fire" (1 Cor 7:9). From another viewpoint the disciples, shaken by learning of the indissolubility of marriage, say to Jesus, "If that is the case of a man with his wife, it is better not to marry" (Matt 19:10). Indeed, neither Christian celibacy nor Christian marriage is fully comprehensible outside the light of faith. Christian virginity is for the Kingdom, and is an authentic love of Christ; Christian marriage draws its strength and ideal from the love of Christ for his Church. A marriage without love is a hell, and virginity without love is a wasteland. Neither one is Christian.

This is why the Second Vatican Council asks that youth receive suitable and timely instruction "above all in the heart of their own families, about the dignity of married love, its role and its exercise; in this way they will be able to en-

Living the love of Christ deep within conjugal reality

Preparing young people for their responsibility

129

gage in honorable courtship and enter upon marriage of their own" (*Gaudium et Spes,* 49).

When death takes a spouse

The fiancés promise fidelity to each other "for the rest of their lives." The day will arrive when one of the spouses will rejoin the Lord whom he or she served during life, allowing the remaining partner to remarry. Such a second marriage might even be desirable for him, for her, or for the good of the children. In addition, the Church has always looked favorably upon celibacy for the sake of the Kingdom. From its beginnings it has respected widowhood. If someone believes that it is better to remain alone, the Church fully respects such a choice. The Church is a true mother who understands what her children go through in their hearts and offers understanding and encouragement as the need arises.

The marriage of non-Christians

Christians have great respect for the marriage of unbaptized persons. Wherever husband and wife love each other faithfully their whole life long, Christians perceive the promise that the covenant between Christ and his Church fulfills. With this kind of fidelity, non-Christians are close to the Kingdom of God.

Civil law and Church law

The laws of some countries demand that a wedding ceremony before a representative of civil authority precede the religious wedding ceremony. But the Church does not recognize the sacrament of marriage in the civil ceremony. It is only through sacramental marriage in the Church that baptized people are husband and wife in the Christian community, even if through civil marriage they are already actually married in the eyes of society.

Catholics who want to marry approach the pastor of their parish some months in advance. They do likewise when the other party is non-Catholic. Indeed, if the faithful want to remain in communion with the Church, they must comply with the requirements of Church law. In the case of mixed marriages, namely between Catholics and non-Catholics, there are certain requirements that pastors are familiar with.

Christian marriage is indissoluble, but sometimes people enter into a marriage that is not really valid. The concerned parties in such a case were never truly married, at least in the sense that the Church understands marriage. These cases are examined by Church tribunals (diocesan officials). Believers who think they are in such a situation can get advice from a priest, preferably their own pastor.

As regards people who have divorced and remarried in a civil ceremony, the Church understands the complex situation they have to deal with. The Church is always ready to support them, despite the fact that it cannot recognize the second marriage nor welcome them to Eucharistic communion.

The priesthood of the laity functions in everyday life, especially in married life. Thus, in accordance with their proper vocation and sustained by a special sacrament, spouses mutually help each other in conjugal and familial life. Their children are called to become members of God's people; the parents will help them grow in the faith and will cultivate the flowering of any vocation that God might give to a child. It is in the family that spouses and children sanctify themselves and, in turn, sanctify other homes. This is why, since the early centuries, the family has been called the "little Church": it is invited to live in communion and reconciliation, and to bring its mission to the whole Church for the building up and sanctification of the world.

The family: the "little Church" in the world

131

Consecrating Oneself to God in Celibacy

Virginity for the Kingdom: a choice the Church has honored from the beginning

Among the evangelical counsels is "the precious gift of divine grace given to some by the Father to devote themselves to God alone more easily with an undivided heart in virginity or celibacy" (*Lumen Gentium* 42). From the earliest times, the Church has accorded special recognition to virgins. It saw this as a duty, partly because an unmarried girl remaining in the parental home was without any specific social status and because it also wanted, above all, to encourage Christians to allow their daughters to forgo marriage. Such a choice of virginity for the Kingdom provoked outright persecution. The Church commemorates the virgin martyrs who through their deaths witnessed their attachment to their Bridegroom.

St. Paul chose celibacy to serve the gospel.

Paul explains to the Corinthians why he remains unmarried and why he would like everyone to be like him. However, "each has a particular gift from God, one of one kind and one of another" (1 Cor 7:7). He realizes that his vocation is not for everyone and gives only counsel in this regard. Virginity frees the heart for undivided love for the Lord: "An unmarried woman or a virgin is anxious about the things of the Lord, so that she may be holy in body and spirit" (1 Cor 7:34). This attachment to the Lord is a meaningful witness to God's Kingdom. Not having the support of a husband or a wife, those who have chosen celibacy express their hope in the Lord, dead and risen.

Multiplicity and diversity of vocations

Some express their attachment to the Lord in contemplative form. Filled with the Spirit, contemplatives cherish the Word in their hearts. They sing God's praises and utter their human lamentations in community, in their "solitude," or even in the midst of the world. Enlivened by the same Spirit, others seek to lead an apostolic life. They take care of the Body of Christ by dedicating themselves totally to their brothers and sisters, especially to those most destitute. Contemplation of the Lord and love of brethren are at the core of every consecrated life.

One can make a vow of virginity or of celibacy, either privately or publicly, through a formula approved by the Church. Those who may feel called to make this vow can obtain help in their decision from a spiritual counselor.

132

Chastity, poverty, and obedience are three evangelical counsels, i.e., three signs of awaiting the Kingdom. The Church of the apostles learned from Christ to be poor. Called to be with him, it not only practiced a poverty of sharing, in which everyone put everything in common (Acts 2:44), but also learned to follow Christ in his suffering, even unto death on a cross. The readiness to be poor with the poor Christ is the sign of a Church prepared to follow its Lord into death, and certain that with him it will also rise again. While virginity is a sign of the love of the Church for its Spouse, poverty is a sign of unconditional adherence to the Redeemer.

"If you wish to be perfect . . . then come, follow me" (Matt 19:21).

Christ was obedient even unto death: he did not want to do *his* will, but that of his Father. In this regard, the Church has wanted men and women to express their desire to follow the Son of God. Those who take vows of obedience learn the will of God in their lives by obeying the Church. They also express how the Church is a pure gift of the Father and how desirable is the will of God: "Our Father . . . thy will be done on earth *as it is in heaven."*

The evangelical counsels of poverty, chastity, and obedience are addressed to everyone, but certain individuals have a vocation to live them radically, as signs of the Kingdom to come. By their vows, they give witness to how much the Church impatiently awaits the Lord: in their daily lives they give expression to the whole Church's prayer: "Come, Lord Jesus" (Rev 22:20).

Being "a sign" of Christ who calls

Virginity in no way diminishes the dignity of marriage. Nor do poverty and obedience. Religious do not scorn people who hold possessions and who assume responsibilities according to God's will. However, knowing that all people should live as if they owned nothing (1 Cor 7:30), they listen to this Word of the Lord in an absolute sense. They renounce their possessions and their own will. They do not despise them, but they receive the grace to renounce them in order to love the Lord with a totally free heart.

The evangelical counsels take on a more stable nature in religious life. The faithful, whether laity or priests, bind themselves by vows or by other commitments to practice the counsels in the context of a community and in line with a particular spirituality.

Religious profession and the consecration of virgins

The rites of religious profession and of the renewal of vows are not sacraments. They are rooted in baptismal consecration, and they join the entire person to the Eucharistic sacrifice.

The Second Vatican Council has called into new respect the traditional consecration of virgins used in the early Church. The solemn rite by which the bishop establishes her who has chosen to live in the state of virginity, as a consecrated person, is made up of a consecrating prayer and the imposition of hands. Through the consecration by the bishop, the virgin becomes a sign of the Church's love for Christ, her Spouse. The virgin is also a sign of hope for God's people, who await the return of the Lord.

How can we help youths find their vocation?

The entire Christian community, through its witness and vitality, ought to help young people listen to the Lord's call and to answer it.

"For every three children born, it has been observed on this topic, one dies of hunger: everybody knows this. On the other hand, what is less known is that among so many young people who reach maturity, many take the wrong path because no one guides them" (G. Baroni).

Receiving the Sacrament of Holy Orders

All the disciples of Christ, baptized into his death and resurrection, are allied with the mission of the Twelve and of the Church. As members of the Body of Christ, laypeople share, as do bishops and priests, in the unique priesthood of Christ. That is why the whole community of the baptized is priestly:

We are a priestly people.

Like living stones, let yourselves be built into a spiritual house to be a holy priesthood, to offer spiritual sacrifices acceptable to God through Jesus Christ (1 Pet 2:5).

Baptism and confirmation mark Christians for life. The Spirit of the Lord dwells in them and renders them suitable for sharing in the threefold function of priesthood: make the gospel known, share in the celebration of the sacraments and the liturgy, bear responsibility for the totality of the Body of Christ. Wherever the Church is, the whole Body of Christ instructs, consecrates, and guides its members:

"But you are 'a chosen race, a royal priesthood, a holy nation, a people of his own, so that you may announce the praises' of him who called you out of darkness into his wonderful light" (1 Pet 2:9).

We exercise our priesthood in everything that we do with love, offering our very selves "as a living sacrifice" (Rom 12:1), whether we offer the Eucharistic sacrifice or witness to Christ in our families and where we work and play.

Priests of the Old Covenant conducted the worship of God by offering animals. In this way they expressed the people's devotion to its God; yet these multiple sacrifices did not succeed in obtaining for human beings either remission of sins or grace. Christ offered himself throughout his whole life to the Father and to humanity with unfailing faithfulness, giving totally of himself even unto death. Christ's sacrifice went on every day, an absolute sacrifice. Now he is our lone mediator with the Father. The common priesthood of all the baptized differs from that of bishops and priests, yet each one shares in the unique priesthood of Christ.

Jesus spoke to the crowds from the lakeshore and many followed them. Going off to the mountain to pray (Mark 6:46), Jesus chose from the crowd twelve disciples whom he

What is the bishop's vocation?

135

joined to himself in a special way. He called them and they were totally at his disposal:

"He went up the mountain and summoned those whom he wanted and they came to him. He appointed twelve . . . that they might be with him and he might send them forth to preach and to have authority to drive out demons . . ." (Mark 3:13-15).

He "appointed twelve," and he established them as a "church" headed by Peter (John 21:15-17). He chose them as his companions and sent them forth. These two aspects still characterize bishops today, as well as priests, who are their assistants: they have a special tie with Christ and are sent by him, just as the Father has sent the Son (John 17:18).

To be with Christ means to follow him. It is in union with Christ that bishops guide God's people and lead believers on the path of the Son to the Father. Sent by Christ and filled with the Holy Spirit, they receive a threefold mission: to evangelize, i.e., to bring new disciples to the Lord and to teach them; to sanctify the faithful and to assemble them in prayer and liturgy, especially the Eucharist; to guide them as shepherds who lay down their lives for their flock.

A grace for all the people of God The ordination of a bishop is a special occasion for the whole Church, for since we are going to the Father's house, we are going there united as the people of God. This union of fellowship centers around the person of Christ, the only Shepherd and Mediator between God and humanity. Insofar as he receives the fullness of the sacrament of orders, the bishop represents Christ in the midst of his people—"head of the body, the church" (Col 1:18). That is why there is

136

no bishop without the people and no people without the bishop. "Wherever I may be," said St. John Chrysostom before going into exile, "you are there too: the body does not sever itself from the head, nor the head from the body. If we are separated by distance, we are united by charity, and even death cannot cut this tie. If my body dies, my soul . . . will remember my people."

Seeing the crowds, Jesus took pity on them because they were like sheep without a shepherd. He then said to his disciples, "The harvest is abundant but the laborers are few; so ask the master of the harvest to send out laborers for his harvest" (Matt 9:37-38).

After Jesus' resurrection, the Twelve chose Matthias to replace Judas. Later they recognized the mission of the Apostle Paul. Thus, the group of twelve gained successors and added to their number in step with the Church's emerging needs. Bishops are the successors to the apostles and bear a mission to the whole world. In union with the successor of Peter, i.e., the pope, they are the guarantors of the Church's unity, apostolicity, and catholicity.

Bishops: successors to the apostles

In each local Church, the bishop is assisted by elders (or "presbyters," namely priests: Acts 15:6, 22). The priests are the bishops' collaborators; together, they form the "presbyterium" or priesthood; they are united to the bishop "as strings to a lyre" (Ignatius of Antioch). Bishops and priests exercise a sacred ministry that is different from the priesthood of the baptized. At ordination they receive a sacred power to build and lead the priestly people, to celebrate in Christ's place the Eucharistic sacrifice that they offer to God on behalf of the entire people of God (*Lumen Gentium*, 10).

Deacons do not have the power to celebrate the Eucharist. Nevertheless, they have the noble mission of helping the bishop and the priests in the proclamation of the Word, in the liturgy (baptism, marriage, and funeral rites) and in charitable works.

The authority of the Church's ministers is not their own: it comes to them from Christ. It is not exercised "over" the Church but "in" the Church as a service: ". . . let the greatest among you be as the youngest, and the leader as the servant" (Luke 22:26). Each receives the sacrament of apostolic ministry from the hands of the bishop, each according to his order: deacons, priests, or bishops. Ordina-

"Do not neglect the gift you have, which was conferred on you through the prophetic word with the imposition of hands of the presbyterate" (1 Tim 4:14).

tion is conferred upon them during the Mass, between the Liturgy of the Word, which sheds light on their vocation, and the Liturgy of the Eucharist, in which the whole people, united with its pastors, gives thanks to God.

The sacramental sign of the three orders is the laying on of hands and the consecratory prayer that confers the Holy Spirit with a view to the ministry. Just as in baptism and confirmation, ordination confers an indelible character on those who receive this sacrament.

Ordination of a bishop   The bishop-to-be receives the fullness of priesthood in the midst of his people in their cathedral during a Mass concelebrated by several bishops and the whole presbyterium, assisted by deacons. After the Gospel, in the presence of everyone, he is called upon to commit himself to maintaining the apostolic faith; to fulfill the duties of his charge at the service of his people; to proclaim the gospel with faithfulness and without ceasing, to keep the deposit of faith, to work at building the Body of Christ, along with the college of bishops under the authority of the successor of Peter; to guide the people toward salvation with his companions in service, the priests and the deacons; to receive with love those who are in need and to lead back those who are astray; to pray without ceasing and to fulfill, as appropriate, his priestly function.

After the laying on of hands by each bishop, an apostolic gesture par excellence, the principal consecrator recites the consecratory prayer while placing the open Book of the Gospels on the ordinand's head. This rite indicates that the bishop is subject to the gospel in his whole ministry. Several complementary rites express the mystery that is taking place. The consecrated bishop is anointed on the head and is given the Book of the Gospels and the insignia of his mission: the ring, symbol of fidelity (*"With faith and love protect the bride of God, his holy Church"*), and the crosier or shepherd's staff, the sign of his responsibility. At this point the bishop is seated on the episcopal chair and presides over the Eucharist in the midst of his people.

Ordination of priests   The future priests receive the priesthood as collaborators of the bishop and members of the presbyterium. The whole ordination rite sheds light on this relationship. The candidate commits himself to collaborate with the bishop to serve and guide the people of God under the leadership of the Holy Spirit; to proclaim the gospel and to celebrate the

138

sacraments according to the tradition of the Church for the praise of God and for the sanctification of the Christian people; to unite himself daily with Christ, who offers himself daily for us to his Father, and to dedicate himself with Christ to God and to human beings; finally, he promises to live in communion with the bishop in respect and obedience.

The bishop then passes on the mission that he himself has received: he confers the sacrament by laying his hands on each ordinand. The assisting priests silently perform the same gesture to signify the entry of the new priest into the presbyterium. The bishop recites the consecratory prayer, then he anoints the hands of the consecrated one in order that he might sanctify the people and offer the Eucharistic sacrifice to God. The bishop hands him the insignia of his mission: the chalice filled with wine and the paten holding bread:

"Accept from the holy people of God the gifts to be offered him. Know what you are doing, and imitate the mystery you celebrate: model your life on the mystery of the Lord's cross."

The new priest then concelebrates for the first time with the bishop and the other priests.

Those who are preparing for the priesthood are first ordained as deacons. Yet the diaconate can also be conferred independently of the priesthood. It is then called the "permanent diaconate."

Ordination of deacons

The Latin Church chooses its permanent deacons from among both celibate and married men. One who is not married commits himself, at the ordination, before God and the Church, to remain celibate for his whole life: *"In accepting out of love the demands of this state, you will show your availability to all people and through your life you will give witness that God ought to be loved more than anything."*

For the married candidate, the bishop requires the consent of his wife: *"Are you resolved to help your husband continue to grow in faith and to support his desire to serve the Church in the order of deacons?"*

The candidate commits himself to carry out his mission with charity and simplicity of heart, to keep the mystery of faith intact and to proclaim it in word and deed, to be faithful to prayer, and to conform his life to Christ's, whose Body

139

and Blood he will distribute to believers. He promises to live in communion with the bishop in respect and obedience.

After the imposition of hands, the bishop pronounces the consecratory prayer. He then hands the Book of the Gospels to the deacon: *"Take care to believe the Word that you will read, to teach what you have believed, to live what you will teach."*

The prayer of the assembly   Deacons, priests, and bishops all owe their vocations to Christ's call, addressed to them personally. This is why, during their ordination and after their promises, they prostrate themselves on the floor. The entire assembly, *"with all the saints who intercede for us,"* commends them to the mercy of God, who has chosen them and who sends them forth.

Liturgical Time

Waking times, watches, calendars, agendas, schedules, timetables, time-wasting, stress . . . We have reached a level of making time into a tyrannizing entity outside of ourselves. In reality, time is a dimension of human life that has also been redeemed by Christ.

In the liturgy, the Christian does not try to get beyond time. On the contrary. In taking on our mortal condition, the Son of God submitted to our time and transfigured it. He gave it back its meaning, its orientation toward God, since even death, which puts an end to our time, leads to the resurrection.

Time for Christians and the Church is inhabited from within by the mysteries that we celebrate, that is, the divine and human stages of salvation history. We live these mysteries (Christmas, Easter . . .) even today, through Christ and in the Spirit. It is in this sense that we speak of a liturgical year; a time punctuated by celebrations and feasts that usher us into the actuality of salvation. "Today, Christ is born. . . . Today, the Spirit is given to us."

Why has God entered our time-frame?

141

The liturgical calendar took shape over centuries. It includes the seasons of Lent, Easter, Advent, Christmas, the time called "Ordinary," and all the feasts of the saints.

Sunday, the weekly Easter

The essential rhythm of the liturgical year is based on the Sunday celebration. Before Easter became a solemn feast, the early Christians gathered each first day of the week to "break bread" (Acts 20:7). Thus, since apostolic times, each Sunday is a weekly celebration of the death and resurrection of the Lord.

The yearly Easter and paschal triduum

The feast of Easter was solemnized beginning with the Council of Nicaea (325). It was set near the Jewish Passover, for the first Sunday after the first full moon of spring. Around this solemnity the paschal triduum was promptly organized, namely three days marked by great liturgies: on Holy Thursday we commemorate the institution of the Eucharist; on Good Friday, we celebrate the Lord's Passion (on this day we fast); on Holy Saturday, without any celebration apart from the office, we meditate on the mystery of Christ laid in the tomb. But at the Easter Vigil, the Church watches with love, listens to the Word of the Lord, and welcomes the newly baptized to its bosom. On that night we celebrate the Lord's resurrection and our passage with him from death to life. This is why we renew our baptismal promises during the Vigil.

Eastertide

On the night and the day of Easter, the joyful baptized people extol the praises of God. The paschal candle lights up the darkness, communicating its light to all believers. Joy and exultation resound in the alleluia that is repeated without end. This acclamation, which means "praise God," is the song of triumph for the redeemed. The mystery of our salvation is so rich that the Church decided to prolong its celebration for seven weeks, at the end of which we celebrate Pentecost (which means fifty). Fifty days after eating the Passover meal, the Hebrew people celebrate the "feast of Weeks," or of the harvest, commemorating the giving of the Law on Sinai. The Christian Pentecost is the culmination of the paschal season. On Pentecost we celebrate the coming of the Holy Spirit upon Mary and the apostles and upon the Church.

Ten days before Pentecost, we celebrate the Ascension of the Lord to the Father. The feasts of Easter, Ascension, and Pentecost are three phases of the one paschal mystery in which we have a share. Having died for the salvation of

142

the world, risen again, and seated at the right hand of the Father, Christ now gives us his Spirit who sends us forth on our mission.

Lent is a time of great spiritual importance for the Church and for each Christian. It is rooted in the biblical tradition of the Exodus, when God, after freeing his people from slavery, purified them during forty years in the desert before bringing them into the Promised Land. It fits within the dynamic of all the other exoduses, both interior and exterior, where the voices of the prophets resound. It connects us as well with the forty days that Jesus spent in the desert in fasting and prayer. During this period the catechumens, accompanied by the Christian community, prepare themselves for the solemn celebration of their baptism. We respond to the Church's pressing appeal that we be converted, that we listen actively to the Word, and that we pray and share our goods. In this way we prepare ourselves for the feast of Easter, but above all for living the paschal mystery every day.

Preparing for Easter

Ash Wednesday opens this period with the distribution of ashes and a fast, not only for penance but also for conversion and sharing. Eight days before Easter we celebrate Palm Sunday. We proclaim the Gospel of the Passion of our Lord, after having recalled his triumphal entry into Jerusalem, which foreshadowed the triumph of Easter. The blessed palms that we carry home to make crosses remind us that Jesus was acclaimed by "the mouths of infants and nurslings" (Matt 21:16).

The feast of Christmas was solemnized around the year 300. It is set on December 25, on or about the day of the winter solstice, when the nights are at their longest; the Savior has come into our night, since he is "the light [that] shines in darkness" (John 1:5).

Feast of the Lord's Nativity

The solemnity of the Nativity of the Lord lasts for eight days, at the end of which we honor Mary, the Mother of God (New Year's Day on our calendar). Shortly afterwards the Sunday of the Epiphany is, in a way, a second celebration of the Lord's Nativity; certain Eastern Churches celebrate Christmas on January 6. Indeed, Jesus' birth, which occurred in lowliness and poverty, is no less than the manifestation of the Son of God to all humanity. This "manifestation" (the meaning of the word *epiphany*) to all the peoples is signified by the Magi from the East.

Christmastide

143

On the following Sunday we commemorate the Baptism of Jesus. This concludes Christmastide, which leaves us with the mystery of the hidden life that Jesus led until the day he began his public life. On that day, he was anointed by the Holy Spirit, and the words of the Father still resound today: "This is my beloved Son" (Matt 3:17).

Preparing for Christmas

The four weeks preceding Christmas make up the time of Advent, a word that evokes the approach of a king or his joyous entry into a town. This period of conversion prepares us for December 25, but, above all, it causes us to lift our eyes toward the Lord who continues to draw near and whose glorious return we await. In a way it is always Advent: the prophets call upon us even today to be vigilant and full of hope. Do we not pray every day, "Our Father . . . thy Kingdom come"?

The Advent season invites us to accept both the Word and God's grace as Mary did, with a totally open heart. As we prepare the crèche, where the Infant Jesus will be placed on Christmas night, we also prepare ourselves in the Church to welcome him about whom we sing, "Christ has come . . . Christ will come again . . . Christ is here."

Ordinary Time

After the seasons of Christmas and Easter, we pass through a long period, the meaning of which we should well understand. "Ordinary" time does not mean "trite" time, i.e., time without importance or significance. On the contrary, it is the time for sowing and for steadfast patience, when we listen to the parables and meditate on Scripture, page by page. It is a time of daily love, a time when the sown seed pushes day by day through the good earth.

This long period is marked by some feasts: at the beginning, the solemnity of the Trinity (Sunday after Pentecost), then the feast of Corpus Christi (the Body of Christ in the Blessed Sacrament); at the end of Ordinary Time, there is the feast of All Saints (November 1) and the commemoration of all the faithful departed, All Souls Day (November 2). On the last Sunday of Ordinary Time we celebrate Christ the King. The new liturgical year begins the following Sunday with the season of Advent.

With Mary, the Church turns toward Christ . . .

Mary is honored often during the year, since she is the first of the redeemed, the first believer, the one through whom the Savior was given to us. By her words she helped with the beginnings of the Church. She intercedes with her Son,

144

Madonna. Joseph O'Connell. Wood and iron. 48'' high. St. Michael's Church, St. Cloud, Minnesota.

with whom she is completely united. In her the Church contemplates its future.

Four of the Marian feasts celebrate the main stages of a life full of grace:

- Immaculate Conception (December 8)
- Annunciation (March 25)
- Mary, Mother of God (January 1)
- Assumption (August 15).

The liturgical year is further punctuated by feasts of saints, who invite us to endure in the faith: "Therefore, since we are surrounded by so great a cloud of witnesses, let us rid ourselves of . . . sin that clings to us and persevere in running the race . . . while keeping our eyes fixed on Jesus'' (Heb 12:1-2).

. . . in the communion of saints.

145

The Church proclaims the paschal mystery in the saints who have suffered with Christ and are glorified with him; it displays their example to the faithful, and through their merits obtains the blessings of God (*Sacrosanctum Concilium,* 104).

The saints were men and women of prayer and penitence. All were "seized" by God and followed Christ. All of them loved the Church and joyfully and courageously took up the service of their brethren. Their witness is a liberating force in our world. This is why we proclaim God's work in them:

You are glorified in your saints,
for their glory is the
crowning of your gifts.

(*Preface I for the feasts of saints*)

They inspire us by their heroic lives,
and help us by their constant
prayers to be the living
sign of your saving power.

(*Preface II for the feasts of saints*)

Celebrating the Lord in our time

From one end of the liturgical year to another, the lives of scattered Christians are thus imbued with a rhythm of peak periods during which we gather, we communicate in the faith and in prayer, and we sustain each other in our conversion and mission.

The liturgy is implanted in our time. It transfigures our history and our commitments "until we all attain to the unity of faith and knowledge of the Son of God, to mature manhood, to the extent of the full stature of Christ . . ." (Eph 4:13) and become "one body, one spirit in Christ" (Eucharistic Prayer III).

Part III
Living
the Gospel

Acting with a Christian Conscience

Living the Faith Today

Do technical and moral progress advance together?

Millions of women and men contribute to social progress, to the development of health, education, and culture. Many commit themselves to justice, build structures for cooperation, or question the world about the radical newness of certain questions: armament, disarmament, relations with the Third World, and bioethical questions. Such moral and spiritual quests are the work of all those who take the future of humanity seriously.

Longing for freedom and liberation is one of the principal signs of the times: freedom of thought, freedom of choice, liberation of the poor and the oppressed. Why does human-

148

ity, as it gradually frees itself through technical, economic, social, and political progress, constantly experience relapses into alienation and see new forms of slavery emerge? From the Christian perspective, there is a connection between God and the desire to be free.

First of all, Christianity is more than a set of rules; it is the Good News. Its originality does not stem from some words of Jesus, but from his life, his death and resurrection, and from the gift of the Spirit. In accepting this mystery, which renews the relationship between human beings and God and the relationships among men and women themselves, the Christian shares in the paschal mystery.

A Christian morality?

It is not merely an individual matter to die to the powers of selfishness and pride by rising with Christ to new life; rather, it is profoundly involved with the future of all humanity. Christian morality is Good News because it allows the human heart to receive the gifts of God: namely, faith, hope, and love.

When Christians read about current events, they view them in light of Scripture; and they approach Scripture according to the manner in which it sheds light on their own lives. They are struck by the way the Bible describes the lives of people, a way that is similar to, yet different from, the accounts in our newspapers and on television news broadcasts.

An optimist because a Christian!

This is understandable since, from the first pages of Genesis, we not only confront the beauty of the world and of humanity, but also human conflict: deception, fratricidal combat, debauchery, chaos in history. For a believer, however, God keeps his promises; something the press never mentions. God gives more and more force to his promises. He has fulfilled them by giving us his Son. And through his Son we know that all of us, even in the depths of sin, enter day by day into a new creation: "Behold, I make all things new," says the Risen Lord to the first Christians devastated by persecution (Rev 21:5). For one who believes, the light shines in the darkness! It is an invitation to live in the light.

People often say to us, "Christians are no better than anyone else!" or "They don't look like they're saved!" True, even after baptism our conversion is not yet complete, and a large part of our existence goes on at a pre-Christian level. Those who are aware of the grace of baptism find themselves continually "on the path of conversion," learning day

What does it mean to live by faith?

by day to put their trust and faith in the Lord more than in themselves alone; the more they trust him, the more they realize who God is, with what love they are loved, and above all, what love really dwells in them.

Faith is more than a call to live in conformity with Christ and the gospel. Since believers trust and accept God's gift, faith really gives them the wherewithal to love with Christ's own love. He who dwells in our hearts works in us and in the world because he is living! He gives us brothers and sisters and ceaselessly gathers all of God's scattered children.

Christian Holiness

What is the purpose of our existence?

To some extent human life resembles life in an anthill. We build societies, we lift up burdens, and we handle problems way beyond our size. That is good, but Scripture tells us: "Unless the Lord build the house, they labor in vain who build it. . . ." (Ps 127:1). And further: "When the Son of Man comes, will he find faith on earth?" (Luke 18:8).

Sainthood is for someone else!

Why are we alive? In the midst of our numerous pursuits, are we really aware that the purpose of our lives is to live in union with God and other human beings in the unity of the Persons in the Trinity?

Christian morality is at the service of this high calling. It is at the service of human life, the purpose of which is holiness and the sanctification of all. St. Paul spoke of the first Christians as "saints!"

Live by the Trinity? I never gave it a thought! Is it for me, personally?

What connection is there between the Trinity and our lives? Why should we look so high? Doesn't this distract us from the real world? God calls us to take our lives seriously. Indeed, through baptism, the Trinity actually dwells in our hearts. Why do we celebrate the love that exists between the Father, the Son, and the Holy Spirit, unless we experience it ourselves? God gives us the ability to praise the Trinity because he gives us life in the perfect love that unites the three Persons.

Isn't it enough to become fully human?

How can we ever love our brothers and sisters, especially our enemies, if we do not draw our love from that of the Father, the Son, and the Holy Spirit? Isn't it an incredible mystery that a human life can carry the divine life, God's whole life, within it? Isn't this the mystery that dwells in the

saints and that sustains the mightiest revolution, the revolution of love?

To live by the grace of baptism, of confirmation, and of the Eucharist is to live by the very love of the Trinity that dwells in us and which, in turn, we give to other human beings. Along with our fellow Christians of the East, we believe that this love "deifies" the human person, that is, it molds him or her into the likeness of God and makes one a child of God.

Christian Morality

Where does Christian morality come from?

Our vocation to holiness is revealed to us by Scripture and by the tradition of the Church. This tradition is alive only when it is welcomed into a living heart.

The Old Testament reveals to us the foundations of spiritual life for human beings by way of a continuous dialogue between God and his people. Among the precepts given by God, the Ten Commandments of Moses, the Decalogue, still guide Christians today. The Old and the New Testaments form a unity. Christians are anchored primarily in the New Testament; but they read the Old Testament in the light of the New.

Compared with the Old Testament, what is new in Christian morality?

"You shall love the Lord, your God, with all your heart . . ." (Deut 6:5) and "You shall love your neighbor as yourself" (Lev 19:18): this fundamental twofold law is the core of the Old Testament. The patriarchs, Moses, the rulers, and the prophets strove to shape their lives by it. By their faith and their love for God's people, they prefigured the Lord and his work of salvation.

In the Old Testament, a neighbor was first of all "a son of [the] people." In the parable of the Good Samaritan (Luke 10:25-37), Jesus reveals to us one new thing: authentic love makes a neighbor out of the other person, whoever he or she is! And then it makes us love that person as ourselves, even if a stranger or an enemy.

The second new thing about Christian behavior lies in the imitation of Christ. To the commandment of loving one's neighbor *as oneself,* a new commandment is added: "As I have loved you, so you also should love one another" (John 13:34).

The Ten Commandments are fulfilled in Jesus, who has

loved us perfectly. It is by this perfect love that we recognize in him the Son of God. "This is how all will know that you are my disciples, if you have love for one another" (John 13:35). This is why Christian behavior has a dimension that is not only individual but also ecclesial: it builds the Church of God.

The Commandments Have Their Source in Life

Moses stated that the precepts of the Law would arouse the admiration of other peoples because of their wisdom (Deut 4:6). He was expressing the hope, still current among Jews and Christians, that the commandments entrusted by God to his people might one day attract other peoples as well.

Everything changes! Is there no constant in morality?

Christian tradition reached the point of speaking about the "natural law," since we believe that every person can recognize in it his or her desire to live as a human being. These precepts are not imposed upon us from outside; they reveal the very meaning of every human life.

The commandments give life (Deut 30:16) to one who observes them, and they assure the unity of God's people who strive to keep them. For a human community to survive, it must be vigilant lest it lapse into false values, into sexuality emptied of its meaning, into injustice that despises humanity. In the same way, the Church cannot survive unless God is acknowledged in it, unless sexuality is correctly expressed, and unless the poor learn the Good News.

Words of life!

The Ten Commandments are for all time and for all people. They are fundamentally immutable, and they are observed all over the world as valid precepts that can be embraced by everyone who strives to do right in his or her life.

The Commandments Seal the Covenant with God

The Ten Commandments are not considered the natural law in the sense that any person could or should discover them just as they are in one's conscience. They are made known to us as having been revealed by God over a long history; they are offered to us as a gift. As Christians, we have received them from the Jewish tradition through our faith in Jesus Christ.

An expression of human awareness or of divine revelation?

We discern the natural law in them in the sense that these Ten Commandments respond to the question of the human conscience: "How should human beings behave in relation to one another and in relation to their creator?"

Morality is not the monopoly of Christians.

We feel ourselves overtaken and even carried along by other currents of morality. This does not shock a Christian, since we are all created in the image of God. The grace of God works in everyone and the Spirit blows where it will.

Every human being is called to the fullness of humanity. As Jews and Christians, we know that this vocation is the gift that God gives us by creating us in his likeness. It is our nature to be what God wants us to be. The words of life are perceived better and better by individuals and peoples to the extent that the sense of Christian values develops in them.

The commandments are like a mirror held up to human nature. They reveal us to ourselves and help us determine how to act in relation to God.

The Ten Commandments

The Bible tells us that Moses presented the Law to the people as a confirmation of the Covenant with God. Yahweh had led his people through the years. From this closeness there arose an ever increasing awareness of the values and demands of life. The Ten Commandments are at once a revelation by God and a discovery by human beings. They have their origin in the history of the salvation that God grants to his people, and they were formulated from within this relationship.

Isn't all this a sign that God and humanity are drawing near each other?

The Book of Exodus describes for us the gift of the Law in the desert at the foot of Mount Sinai. This narrative recounts for us a celebration, the form of which is close to our celebration of the Eucharist. The people first listen to the Law and answer God by proclaiming their loyalty with one voice. Then the Covenant that the Lord has concluded with them is sealed by a sacrificial meal and by sprinkling the people with the blood of the sacrificed animals: "This," said Moses, "is the blood of the covenant" (Exod 24:8). By keeping the commandments, the Israelites show that they want to belong to the people of the Covenant, to the community that God assembles.

Who could have expected such intimacy with God?

In a marvelous passage, upon which the Church meditates in prayer, the Lord speaks to Moses of the intimacy that his Word creates between him and us:

"For this command which I enjoin on you today is not too mysterious and remote for you. It is not up in the sky. . . . Nor is it across the sea. . . . No, it is something very near to you, already in your mouths and in your hearts; you have only to carry it out" (Deut 30:11-14).

Jesus Teaches the Law

Jesus is the bridge between the Old Testament law and the law of the New Testament. He is the new lawgiver who interprets for a new people what Moses had interpreted for the people of the Old Covenant.

In the Sermon on the Mount (Matt 5:1–7:28), Jesus, the new Moses, proclaims on another mountain his way of understanding the commandments. He presents them as the gate-

Did Jesus abolish the commandments?

155

way to the Kingdom of heaven, but he gives them new depth. He does not suppress the words of life, but rather says:

"Do not think that I have come to abolish the law or the prophets. I have come not to abolish but to fulfill. . . . Therefore, whoever breaks one of the least of these commandments and teaches others to do so will be called least in the kingdom of heaven. But whoever obeys and teaches these commandments will be called greatest in the kingdom of heaven" (Matt 5:17-19).

Attitude? What attitude?

Yet he also states that keeping these commandments must go beyond the faithfulness to the law as practiced by certain members of the Chosen People: "I tell you, unless your righteousness surpasses that of the scribes and Pharisees, you will not enter the kingdom of heaven" (Matt 5:20). The love that Jesus preaches is not primarily the fruit of personal effort in view of some reward, but is a free collaboration with the will of God that was manifested long before our own. There is no need to wait for love from somebody else in order to respond to it:

". . . be children of your heavenly Father, for he makes his sun rise on the bad and the good, rain to fall on the just and the unjust." If one wishes to become a child of such a Father, it is necessary, with the same unconditional freedom, to take the initiative in loving the other person. The stranger and even the enemy invite us to form with them a community and to build the Church of God (Matt 5:43-48).

Following the Path of the Beatitudes

Happy are the poor and those who weep. Really?

Jesus' teaching in the Beatitudes is a new explication of the Mosaic Law. Not only is Jesus the fulfillment of that law, but he brings continuity to it, as he tells us how to understand it.

An earthly taste of the happiness of the world to come is what the Lord offers us. The Beatitudes open the Sermon on the Mount (Matt 5:1-12). They outline the characteristics of the love by which the new community lives. They act as invitations to an authentic Christian life.

Jesus turns the world upside down.

The poor in possessions and in heart are happy because they rely on Providence and on God's help more than on their own resources or their personal abilities. The Kingdom of heaven already belongs to them!

Humble of heart and aware of their unworthiness, the meek are happy; since they are patient and kind, "they will inherit the land."

Happy are those who weep because of oppression and injustice; happy also are those who weep over their sins, for the tears of repentance give them the spiritual joy of children once lost but now found. "They will be comforted."

Those who hunger and thirst for justice are happy to share in the will of God and to promote justice. "They will be satisfied."

Happy are the merciful, those who know how to forgive. They will be freed from spitefulness and rancor. "They will be shown mercy."

Happy are the pure in heart, those who in the depths of their being do not dwell on doing evil, because they clearly distinguish between good and evil: "They will see God."

Happy are those who sow peace: poor, humble, meek, thirsting for justice and pure in heart. "They will be called children of God."

Blessed are those who are persecuted for the sake of Christ, for their reward is great in heaven! To deny Christ is the most dramatic sin. To suffer for Christ is the most glorious witness of faithfulness and love that human beings can render to the Lord who died for them.

On Pentecost, God sent us the Holy Spirit. In a sense, the Spirit continues Jesus' work on earth, since it is the Spirit working in and among us that makes God's work our own.

The gifts of the Spirit are fruitful. They multiply like the talents in the parable (Matt 25:14-30) when they are in good hands. They build the kingdom of God.

In contrast to passing realities, faith, hope, and love remain; they bring us into the ultimate community. Inspired by the spirit of the Beatitudes, St. Paul speaks out his jubilation:

"Love is patient, love is kind. It is not jealous, love is not pompous, it is not inflated, it is not rude, it does not seek its own interests, it is not quick-tempered, it does not brood over injury, it does not rejoice over wrongdoing but rejoices with the truth. It bears all things, believes all things, hopes all things, endures all things. Love never fails" (1 Cor 13:4-8).

Forming One's Conscience in the Church

Every Christian must act according to his or her conscience, but conscience needs to be informed by the law.

St. Paul gives the example of Christians who do not dare to eat meat that has been offered to idols. We can use the example of those who still believe in conscience that they may not eat meat on Friday: they are mistaken. However, if they do eat meat while believing that they are sinning against the law of the Church, then they really do sin. Indeed, the Christian must follow his or her conscience, even when it is wrong. We should then correct the conscience of those who believe they sin by eating meat on Friday, so that they might understand that the Church no longer obliges us to observe meatless Fridays. The mature Christian, however, may choose to abstain from meat as an act of self-denial, i.e., something one purposely seeks to do rather than something one is asked or told to do.

As a Christian, is my conscience individualistic or social?

Let us continue with our example. As long as our fellow Christians persist in this error, we may not entice them into eating meat on Friday. The sensitivity of a conscience that belongs to a friend obliges us to respect that friend's erroneous conscience. Paul writes, ". . . if food causes my brother to sin, I will never eat meat again, so that I may not cause my brother to sin!" (1 Cor 8:13). Those who fol-

low their conscience, even if it is informed, must always act as a brother or sister in faith, and not as a freethinker: "When you sin in this way against your brothers and wound their consciences, weak as they are, you are sinning against Christ" (1 Cor 8:12). The mature Christian will feel obliged to lead the immature.

Any Christian who understands the demands of Christian morality has the duty of explaining them to someone who does not. Further, by teaching each other we build Christian community and save one another from sin:

". . . if anyone among you should stray from the truth and someone bring him back, he should know that whoever brings back a sinner from the error of his way will save his soul from death and will cover a multitude of sins" (James 5:19-20).

While is it true that each person must follow his or her conscience, each is bound in conscience to become informed so as not to act blindly. Following one's conscience does not mean being subjective or "doing what one feels like";

Moral carelessness?

159

following one's conscience means discovering the serious moral requirements of one's personal life and vocation and taking personal responsibility for assuming them. By speaking and acting incorrectly, one can also be an occasion for the fall of others. Each one then is responsible for any error in his or her conscience and for the carelessness that it reflects.

To become better informed, a Christian humbly sets about to listen to the Word of God, to the church community, and to the human community. Conscience does not establish the law but receives it from God and from human society. Thus, doing away with Friday abstinence does not indicate carelessness! On the contrary, a Christian is called upon to take up the Church's concern for promoting an authentic sense of penance: I am no longer bound to deprive myself of meat on Friday in compliance with a rule; however, I am invited to select a privation (of food or something else), freely and out of love, on days when, with the whole Church, we call to mind the Lord's death.

"Love, and do what you will"
(St. Augustine).

In small actions as well as in important choices, the Christian's wakened conscience becomes more and more attentive to the guiding words of Christ and the Church. It learns to respond better and better, with an ever more authentic love, to the demands of the situation. It studies all aspects of a problem without prejudice or narrowmindedness.

Little by little, the Christian conscience acts like a compass of love. St. Augustine says that when one has matured in the love of Christ and the Church, one can act according to one's heart, and one will act well. This compass of love is the movement of the Spirit of Jesus, the Holy Spirit who dwells in us and who puts our heart at ease and frees it.

Is the law contrary to my freedom?

The law does not make slaves of us. On the contrary, it contributes to freeing us from our ignorance and recklessness. It invites us to live in the Church and in solidarity with all people. It makes free beings out of us by liberating us from our self-centeredness. It is in this context that each one of us can determine our motives and in good conscience decide if the law applies in this or that concrete life situation. The law, then, does not suppress individual responsibility.

And what if my conscience comes
into conflict with the law?

Certain laws, formulated by society in keeping with time and place, can conflict with a decision that a conscientious Christian deems necessary to make. The Christian should then adopt an honest and adult attitude and consider the challenge that the law presents. Even though there may be some merit to following the dictates of one's conscience, one is nevertheless responsible for informing his or her own conscience.

Certain laws of society, however, can prove to be truly unjust, for example, in medical, social, or political areas; in such a case, the Christian may well be obliged not to obey them.

Remorse and Awareness of Sin

As the day ends, sometimes a feeling of deep satisfaction comes upon us: the day was good, the work well done. Then again, perhaps some shadow disturbs this contentment, or the memory of some fault arouses a bad feeling in us. Is this kind of "regret" the sign of true guilt? Not really, since a fault is not necessarily a sin. To commit a *fault* is to deviate with respect to an objective norm or an ideal that one has assumed. It is to miss an envisioned objective. Such a shortcoming can cause resentment that can feel like guilt: one has the feeling of not being truly good, even of being good for nothing.

Is a bad conscience a good counselor?

To commit a *sin* is to do something evil, knowingly and willingly. A sin is more than a fault: it damages one's relationships with God, with others, and with oneself. It wounds persons in their very heart and soul.

Remorse is not the sign of an acute sense of sin, but is the expression of a kind of disquiet that arouses concern over oneself. It is important to distinguish clearly between remorse or mere uneasiness and true contrition. In an overly strict conscience there is an excess of perceived guilt about the real extent of the fault. The vexation, tied to reflecting on oneself, is accompanied by discouragement. It does not open up one's heart toward the person one has harmed; it can even harden it.

How does one go from remorse to contrition?

Real contrition, on the other hand, is a surge of love, an authentic regret of the evil committed toward God or his children. It is a clear view of oneself, with a trust in God, who calls the sinner back and creates him or her anew. Repentance turns the sinner toward the Father and toward others in the quest for forgiveness and in the concern for restoring relationships. True contrition aspires to ultimate reconciliation and is sustained by a firm resolve not to do

161

the same thing again. It is an impulse of the Spirit that makes us cry, "Abba, Father!" It has nothing to do with discouragement. On the contrary, it widens one's heart and opens it to trust. Contrition is the love that is redeemed by Love (God) who grants pardon.

Sinning? What is the real question?

Sin does not take us by surprise. One does not wake up from sin as if from an isolated act that makes one ask, "How could this happen to me?" Rather, the real question is, "How did I come to this?" Sin looms larger in our lives than sudden, everyday faults. Sin lurks in our habits, in the grumbling of our hearts, in the vexation of our souls, and in the

Doesn't every sin have a history?

aberrations of our intelligence. Perhaps someday it comes forth to lead the sinners where their hearts of stone, parched souls, and twisted intelligences wanted them to go. To be reconciled means also to be at peace. It means returning to the grace of one's baptism to find once again a pure heart, a simple soul, and an intelligence steeped in the mystery of the faith.

Venial sin?

Not all sins have the same seriousness, far from it. There are thoughts, words, actions, and omissions that the conscience reproaches. Tradition calls them "venial" sins, meaning "pardonable." They are not mortal, that is, they do not destroy one's relationship with God and the Church. It is good for Christians to remember this in order to reconcile themselves with God and with the Church before they become lost or indifferent.

Mortal sin?

A mortal sin denotes an attitude of heart or behavior that gravely damages relationships with God, with the Church, and with other human beings.

With God and the Church: for example, by abandoning deliberately all recourse to the sacraments (which also means that one excludes oneself from the community); by perverting one's conscience by calling good what is evil, by not being willing to recognize the work of the Spirit where the fruits are evident, and by calling it the work of the Evil One, that is, by blaspheming against the Spirit; by closing oneself willfully to God's teaching; by disfiguring the faith through heresy or through moral indifference; by denying the Lord.

With one's neighbor: by ruining the neighbor with attacks on the person's reputation, possessions, physical or moral being; by destroying a family through adultery or injustice; by seeking to put someone's faith in jeopardy.

162

These sins are not forgivable except through a true sacramental reconciliation, so that the Christian might be readmitted to communion at the Lord's Supper. Indeed, how can someone whose heart destroys love share in the Body and Blood of Christ, which speak of unbounded love? (John 13:1).

Sin and Reconciliation

When converts receive baptism, they need not confess their sins in an exhaustive way, but must renounce fully and sincerely everything sinful in their lives. Baptized in Christ, they die to sin and are reborn to new life. "No one begotten of God sins" (1 John 5:18). Sin is a return to the life of "the former person," a life without faith and without Christ's commandment. One who is living this way must renew his or her conversion and be reconciled through the sacrament of penance, which is like a second baptism.

"Do you renounce Satan, and all his pomps and all his works?"

Very often, those who habitually lead immoral lives lose the sense of sin and guilt altogether. But when the law of Christ is recognized through baptism, sin is identified, and Christians avow their sins by confessing them to the Church.

The commandment of Christ is new because Jesus demands that we build the Church, that is, build the community of disciples based on mutual love among brothers and sisters in the faith. The community ought to be a sign of Christ:

Can people recognize us as the Lord's disciples?

"As I have loved you, so
you also should love one another.
This is how all will know that you are my disciples,
if you have love for one another" (John 13:34-35).

Where believers give witness to an authentic love and radiate Christ's own love, everybody can recognize in them the Lord's disciples. Where the Christian community is inactive and ineffective, and where the love of the Church loses fervor, no one can recognize the disciples of the Lord.

When we neglect this new commandment, we disregard him who gave it to us. On that account, we show contempt for the whole Law. We no longer love the Lord with all our heart, with all our soul, and with all our mind, nor our neighbor as ourselves. We no longer love one another as Christians, as the Lord has loved us. This contempt for the Christian community lies at the root of all other sins.

Isn't love more important than the Church?

163

How shall we approach conversion?

We imagine too easily that to convert oneself means no longer to commit this or that sin. This amounts to reestablishing a balance within oneself and to restoring self-mastery. What a mistake! To be converted means above all to return to the ones we abandoned: to the Christian community and through it to God and to all our brothers and sisters.

This is why it is wise to take advantage of the sacrament of reconciliation. If we have seriously sinned, we are bound to confess ourselves to a priest, who represents the Lord, and to the Christian community as well. To disregard the sacrament of reconciliation is a sign that we do not love the Church enough. Loving this sacrament shows that we care about building the Christian community. Perhaps what is needed is a whole new understanding of just what the idea of reconciliation means in today's world.

The Ten Commandments in the Catholic Tradition

Aren't the Ten Commandments obsolete?

The Ten Commandments, or Decalogue, are the charter laws of God's people. The early Church, issuing from the Hebrew people, made reference mainly to the Sermon on the Mount to draw from it the newness of the gospel and the Beatitudes, and to savor it all. Later on, the Church, which developed in mostly pagan surroundings, felt compelled to recover its roots more explicitly. Since the fourth century, under the influence of St. Augustine, the Ten Commandments constituted part of the catechetical instruction for those seeking baptism and for the faithful. Since the Second Vatican Council, contemporary emphasis has been placed on the gospel in daily life, the role of the Holy Spirit, and the importance of community. Less mention is made of the Ten Commandments; our youngsters must feel that the commandments belong to the "old days."

The time has come to reconsider these ten laws of life, without prejudice and with a humble heart. Jesus himself submitted to them in the love he gave to his Father. He interiorized them and brought them to their perfection.

An asutere formulation

Let us look at the text printed on the following pages (pp. 166–167). On the left is the version from the Old Testament. It comes to us from two very similar traditions taken from Exodus (20:2-17) and from Deuteronomy (5:6-21). The majority of the commandments are formulated in the nega-

164

tive. They follow the style: "You shall not . . . ." Would positive orders like "do this" or "do that" have been less shocking to our sensibilities? Some commandments are accompanied by a short commentary (which we have abridged) to explain their meaning.

On the right-hand page, we recognize the text that many people once learned in their catechism. It is the version that the Church has provided since the sixteenth century, in concise and rhythmic formulas that are easy to memorize.

We compare the Bible with the catechetical text.

In the margin of the traditional Catholic version, we provide a parallel text that corresponds to the numbered commandments as they appear in the next chapter. They explain the meaning of each Old Testament commandment by pointing out its Christian and positive significance.

In the Church's catechetical practice, the listing has not always been the same. Since the time of St. Augustine (354–430), the first and second biblical commandments have been combined into one. Among Catholics and Lutherans, then, the numbering is one digit behind the biblical numbering. For example, the seventh commandment in Scripture and in the Orthodox tradition is our sixth. Again, our ninth and tenth commandments are combined in the Bible. They were separated into two commandments in the Western Christian tradition to correspond to the biblical number of ten.

The Ten Commandments
of the Old Testament

1. **You shall not have other gods besides me.**

2. **You shall not make idols.**
   You shall not bow down before them or worship
     them,
   for I, the Lord, am your God,
   who brought you out of the land of Egypt,
   that place of slavery.
   I am a jealous God.

3. **You shall not take the name of the Lord,**
   your God, in vain.

4. **Remember to keep holy the sabbath day,**
   for the seventh day is the sabbath
   of the Lord, your God.
   No work may be done then either by you,
   or your son or daughter,
   or your male or female slave,
   or by the alien who lives with you.
   Your male and female slave
   should rest as you do.
   For remember that you too were once slaves,
   and the Lord, your God, set you free.

5. **Honor your father and mother,**
   that you may have a long life and prosperity,
   in the land that the Lord, your God,
   is giving you.

6. **You shall not kill.**

7. **You shall not commit adultery.**

8. **You shall not steal.**

9. **You shall not bear false witness against your neighbor.**

10. **You shall not covet your neighbor's house, nor**
    his wife, . . . nor anything that belongs to your
    neighbor.

Catholics & Lutherans combine making & worshipping idols into 1 commandment. The Bible & other Christians separate it into 2 commandments.

Bible & other Christians combine #s 9 & 10. We separate to keep biblical #10.

The Ten Commandments in Catholic Catechesis

1. **You shall adore God, and love him above all.**

   I am your God who has set you free; you shall have no other gods besides me.

2. **You shall revere his holy name, avoiding blasphemy and false oaths.**

   The name of God is holy; you shall not take it in vain.

3. **You shall keep the Lord's Day by serving God with devotion.**

   Every Sunday we celebrate the Lord's Passover.

4. **Honor your father and mother, and likewise your superiors.**

   "Honor your father and your mother, as the Lord, your God, has commanded you" (Deut 5:16).

5. **Avoid killing and scandal, likewise hate and anger.**

   You shall not kill; you shall respect human life.

6. **You shall remain pure in all your actions.**

   You shall not commit adultery; your love shall remain faithful.

7. **You shall not take another's goods, nor keep them unjustly.**

   You shall not enslave or exploit a human being; you shall safeguard each person's freedom and dignity.

8. **You shall reject slander and lying as well.**

   Your witness shall be true; speak well of your neighbor.

9. **You shall stay totally pure in thoughts and desires.**

   You shall remain entirely pure in all thoughts and desires.

10. **You shall not covet your neighbor's goods nor hold them dishonestly.**

    You shall look upon your neighbor without coveting his or her goods; see, rather, what you can share with your neighbor.

The Ten Commandments

1. I am your God who has set you free; you shall have no other gods besides me

The first commandment puts us in the presence of God, who frees us from all slavery; he puts us on our guard against erroneous beliefs.

God is one. There is no other. "I am," said the Lord while revealing himself to Moses in the burning bush. Compared to him, all other gods are only idols.

Is it only a matter of turning away from idols?

Idols neither act nor react: "They have mouths but speak not; they have eyes but see not; they have ears but hear not . . ." (Ps 115:5-6). The God of the Covenant makes everything exist, he sees that what he has made is good; he may speak to the human heart directly or perhaps indirectly through events; he hears the cry of his people and the prayer of the poor; he has "depths of mercy." He is a living God, a God who saves, a person. He speaks to us in terms of "I" and "thou," "thine" and "mine," as between lovers. He makes a covenant. He says, "I am *your* God" (Deut 5:6). He gives himself to us, he walks with his people and leads them on.

When a person lives close to God, he or she becomes "one" with him and in the process becomes "one" in him or herself—a person of integrity. "You shall love the Lord, your God, with all your heart, and with all your soul, and with all your strength" (Deut 6:5). All aspects of the believer's life thus form a coherent unity. How could we then love God "half-way," "dancing with one foot on another," as the prophet Elijah reproached the people unfaithful to God? Is there anything that tears a person apart more than having a double life, a divided heart, serving God and money? (Matt 6:24). What could benefit a person's health more than to have his life unified by the gift of love! The gift of God's love frees one from the idolatry of I/Me, of money, of power, and of sexuality.

"Lord, make me single-hearted!" (Ps 86:11, Jerusalem Bible).

169

In reading the New Testament, we discover that the God of the New Covenant reveals himself as the Father of Jesus Christ, and he gives us his Holy Spirit:

"The Father is God, the Son is God,
the Holy Spirit is God;
nevertheless, they are not three gods,
but one God" (Creed of St. Athanasius).

To believe means to commit oneself in the faith.

The history of the Church is distinguished by men and women who have left all to give themselves to God alone, and whom God has captivated with his love. "You are lacking in one thing. Go, sell what you have . . . then . . . follow me," said Jesus to the rich young man (Mark 10:21).

Even amid worldly cares and in the midst of possessions and responsibilities, everything that is not God is relative and reflects him. St. Teresa of Avila said it best: "Let nothing trouble you. Let nothing distract you. Everything passes. God does not change. Patience can do anything. Be patient for God. You will lack nothing. God alone is enough." St. Teresa's life was committed to prayer and action—committed but not scattered.

The time has come to adore God.

Yahweh says, "I am a jealous God!" (Deut 5:9). Isn't there something shocking about all this? Shouldn't he have said, "I am an indifferent God"? No, like all lovers, God does not put up with rival gods. Nothing is dearer to his heart than our faithfulness. This faithfulness does not come naturally to us. It is begged for in prayer and received in adoration. To adore God is to dwell in his presence; it is to walk in his presence like lovers who, even when separated by distance, do not live or think without the thought of each other. Since they adore each other, the whole life of the one is ordered toward the love of the other, mutually. Through prayer, Christians can direct their whole lives toward God. In adoration they become one with God. In silence they communicate with him, and their hearts expand in joy and praise.

Praises to the Lord

You alone are holy, Lord God,
you who do marvelous things!

You are strong,
You are great,
You are the Most High,
You are the Almighty,
You, Holy Father,
King of heaven and of earth.

You are three
and you are one at the same time,
Lord God, all good,
You are the only good,
You are all good,
You are the sovereign good,
Lord God living and true.

You are charity, love,
You are wisdom,
You are humility,
You are patience,
You are safety,
You are rest,
You are joy and gladness,
You are justice and propriety,
You are richness and wealth.

You are beauty,
You are sweetness,
You are our shelter,
You are our guardian and defender,
You are power,
You are refreshment.

St. Francis. Joseph O'Connell.
Woodcarving. 10" x 10." Francis Spanier
Collection.

You are our hope,
You are our faith,
You are our great sweetness,
You are our eternal life,
great and admirable Lord,
all-powerful God,
sweet merciful Savior.

St. Francis of Assisi

Your Will Be Done on Earth as It Is in Heaven:

Let us love you
with all our heart
by thinking always of you;
with all our soul
by desiring you always;
with all our spirit
by directing all our impulses toward you
and by pursuing nothing but your glory;
with all our powers
by consuming all our energies
and all the senses of our soul and our body
in the service of your love and nothing else.
Let us love our neighbors as ourselves,
by attracting all of them to your love as far as we
are able. . . .

St. Francis of Assisi

"You shall [make] no idol . . ."
(Deut 5:8-10).

The second biblical commandment, which Christian catechesis has combined with the first, prohibits us from making representations of God after our image, as pagans do. We do not have our God "in hand" at our command, as in superstitious practices. He is "in heaven!"

Images tell us about God, but they are not God. When we venerate statues, crucifixes, and icons, it is because we seek to approach an invisible God through a visible work of art.

Preaching what we imagine

It is possible that our faith becomes fixed on the concept of an imaginary god whom we make to the measure of our intelligence or our likeness. What is more harmful to love than to reduce the other to oneself? We are all affected by our desires, our fears, our cultural heritage, and our rational projections.

"[Christ] is the image of the invisible
God" (Col 1:15).

"God is manifest in Jesus Christ. He showed himself to us as he is, vulnerable in love. And yet in Jesus we have seen his glory . . . coming from the Father" (John 1:14). God is manifest in his Son, but few have recognized him, except for the lowly and the humble of heart. "I give praise to you, Father, Lord of heaven and earth, for although you

172

have hidden these things from the wise and the learned you have revealed them to the childlike,'' said Jesus (Matt 11:25). Christ is ''the image of the invisible God,'' wrote St. Paul. He is the ''icon'' that makes God present. Besides Jesus, no other image is God.

2. *The name of God is holy; you shall not take it in vain*

The second commandment does not speak to us about other gods or about idols or images, but about the Name. The name of God designates the very *person* of God: So that at the name of Jesus every knee should bend, of those in heaven and on earth and under the earth . . . (Phil 2:10).

Sanctifying the name of God

The Christian is happy to talk about God and does not blush at it. He loves it when his whole life speaks of God, following Paul's recommendation to Timothy: ''Let no one have contempt for your youth, but set an example for those who believe, in speech, conduct, love, faith, and purity . . . attend to the reading, exhortation, and teaching. Do not neglect the gift you have . . .'' (1 Tim 4:12-14).

We live ''*in the name* of the Father, and of the Son, and of the Holy Spirit.'' We invoke the ''name'' of God, we praise him, we proclaim him. The name ''makes him present.'' This is why we pronounce the name of God with respect when we proclaim his Word in our liturgies and when we praise the Lord, ''Hallowed be thy name!'' The Lord's name is beautiful. Even alone, it is a prayer to him.

To those disciples who were not sincerely conforming their lives to the gospel, Jesus directed this warning: ''Not everyone who says to me, 'Lord, Lord,' will enter the kingdom of heaven, but only the one who does the will of my Father in heaven. Many will say to me on that day, 'Lord, Lord, did we not prophesy in your name? Did we not drive out demons in your name? Did we not do mighty deeds in your name?' Then I will declare to them solemnly, 'I never knew you. Depart from me, you evildoers'' (Matt 7:21-23).

To invoke God's name is not enough.

To swear, to take an oath, means to call God as a witness, attesting that what one says is true and that what one promises will be kept! Thus in these important commitments we render homage to God, the source of truth, and we appeal to his faithfulness. On the contrary, when we call God as a witness through a false oath, we are using his name

Calling God as a witness

to mask lies and infidelity. And when, before God, we take an oath lightly, we fail in truth and justice toward him.

"Let your 'Yes' mean 'Yes,' and your 'No' mean 'No.' Anything more is from the evil one" (Matt 5:37).

To blaspheme is to blame God in an outburst of despair or bitterness, with the deliberate purpose of rejecting him. In the Bible, surely, the psalms are filled with cries of distress: "Lord, why have you done this to me? Do you no longer care for me?" But these cries are a prayer that the Church makes its own every day. It is one thing to turn toward God and another thing to say: "God did this to me! God no longer takes care of me!" . . . This "God" is no longer part of an "I/Thou" relationship, and is accused with a contempt that, after a while, can be lethal to the faith.

3. Every Sunday we celebrate the Lord's Passover

The third commandment is concerned with the Lord's Day, the Sunday Eucharist, and refraining from work in the Lord's honor. For the Christian, Sunday is not the last day of the week, but the first. The Risen Christ brings to it the newness of the Easter life. This day is an invitation to live in the three great dimensions of Christian life: faith, hope, and love.

Celebrating the Lord's Day: an act of faith

Every Sunday, the Risen Christ calls us together to celebrate, in the Church, the memorial of his Passover, i.e., his passing over from death to life. Those who regularly and purposely withdraw from this summons end up by no longer nourishing their life in faith. They lose contact with their sisters and brothers and stubbornly neglect not only the Lord's call but also the fact that the Lord gives himself to them as nourishment. Sharing in the Eucharist is a duty and a vital necessity. Without the Mass, after a while faith perishes in the Christian's heart, and the community is made poorer.

The Sunday rest is also an act of faith. To refrain from work is to believe that this life, which is a gift of God, can continue, even if we stop worrying and working on that day. In accepting this time to rest, we tell the Lord that he is at the source of our lives and that he frees us from all slavery, even sometimes from the slavery of work.

On Sunday, resurrection day, we live our hope for the Lord's return more intensely, and we make ours the call of the Church: "Come, Lord Jesus!" (Rev 22:20). The birth pangs of this world are nothing compared to the new life that irresistibly grows to perfection, or compared to the expectation of our resurrection by the end of time. In celebrating the Eucharist, we proclaim the Lord's resurrection and we await his coming in glory.

The Lord's Day is "holy," which means that it is a special day—out of the ordinary—a foretaste of ultimate life. It is not a day for catching up with the time we lost the previous week, or for accumulating energy for the work ahead; nor is it a day on which we allow ourselves to be dominated by the leisure industry. The foretaste of eternity that marks this day dares us to show ourselves as being more human and more Christian.

Christ gives himself over to us in the Eucharist so that we might give of ourselves as he offered himself, body and

Celebrating Sunday: a source of charity

blood. Through contacts among Christians and through announcements made at the Sunday celebration, we share the joys and pains of the parish and of the whole community. We support the needs of the world in the prayer of the faithful. Through the collection, we give practical witness of our love for those in need: ". . . God loves a cheerful giver" (2 Cor 9:7).

Sunday retains the value of the sabbath: "You were slaves of Pharaoh," said God, "but I made you free. . . ." The sabbath, however, does not paralyze all human activity. Indeed, it was on the sabbath that Jesus healed a man with a paralyzed hand, for ". . . the sabbath was made for man, not man for the sabbath" (Mark 2:27). Thus, those who provide various services on Sundays (hospitals, public transport, restaurants . . .) contribute to the freedom of their brothers and sisters. That is why Christians should be concerned for service personnel and protect them from exploitation. Sunday, of all days, should call for a more equitable distribution of work among people.

The celebration of Sunday is a source of human and social renewal. It implies that fellowship extends throughout the whole week. In Christ, every human being is our brother or sister. Celebrating the Lord's Day is a call to change society, its mentality and its systems. In this way, Sunday can truly be called the *first* day of the week.

Let Sunday be a feast!

To live in the love of the ecclesial community of the home, to take time to be with others, to celebrate an event, to pay a visit or write a letter to someone who is alone or far away, to relax, to begin and renew relationships in relaxation, to be interested in what is happening in the world, and to admire beauty—all this gives color to our lives.

4. "Honor your father and your mother, as the Lord, your God, has commanded you" (Deut 5:16)

Honor?

The fourth commandment is about respect for different generations. Without our parents and our ancestors, we would not exist.

The Lord demands that children and adults honor their father and mother. To "honor" them means to grant them the importance they deserve. This importance is due them

for their love, their work, their devotion, and simply the fact that they transmitted life to us, life that comes from God.

As they approach adulthood, young people acquire autonomy. At this stage, teenage hurts and problems are inevitable. The passage to adult independence suffers crises of growth that force parents and children toward mutual recognition. When youths achieve true autonomy and can freely live their own lives, parental authority has fulfilled its goal. In this gradual development, parental authority diminishes and the youths' respect for them grows.

Authority is mainly a service. Didn't Jesus say, "Let the greatest among you be as the youngest, and the leader as the servant" (Luke 22:26)? All true authority presupposes mutual understanding: that of the elders with the richness of their experience and that of the young people with their fresh view on life and society. Listening to one another aids and abets a gradual sharing of responsibilities.

Authority above all?

The authority of parents belongs to the father and the mother. Family life ultimately affects society-at-large. Men and women together bear responsibility for the family and for humanity.

Respect for those who exercise authority goes beyond the family context. A people—a society or a Church—cannot cut themselves off from their heritage lest they lose their own vitality. To acknowledge only the achievements of the present and to reject the contributions of those who have gone before us will certainly leave us poorer.

Christian tradition carries with it an experience of faith. Under the influence of the Holy Spirit, it expresses itself creatively in doctrine, liturgy, and morality. The role of authority is to promote the dynamism and richness of this tradition. Accordingly, we speak of a living tradition.

Doesn't all authority come from God?

To exercise authority means to promote life and true liberty, whether individual or collective. The source of this task lies in God. According to Scripture, God casts blame on those who exercise authority for the sake of absolute power. They refuse to open themselves and submit to the Word and to God's liberating action. For this reason, in certain cases "we must obey God rather than men" (Acts 5:29).

Respect for parents and for those in authority is not based primarily on their abilities or personal merits, but upon certain parental or social responsibilities. Mutual respect involves an element of forgiveness and reconciliation. Children, young people, and all who are subject to authority are called upon to pray for parents and for all who hold responsible positions in society and in the Church. Indeed, authority and peace are not brought about by human effort alone. They are gifts from God.

St. Paul gives us a very balanced exhortation: "Children, obey your parents in the Lord." "Fathers, do not provoke your children to anger," but bring them up with the training and instruction of the Lord (Eph 6:1-4).

These days we are more aware of the situations that strain relations between parents and children, especially housing conditions, work, unemployment, and health (physical, mental, and moral). Therefore, Christians should strive all the more to humanize living conditions for all families.

The fourth commandment concerns not only the respect of children toward their parents but, likewise, the respect of parents toward their children.

178

Parents are the links in the long chain of religious tradition. They are the first catechists for their children. They tell the story of God's love, its accomplishments, and its obstacles among human beings. They do this by being what they are, very simply by "practicing what they preach." The mutual love between parents is the soul and measure of all their efforts at raising children. Without love, the finest rules of upbringing cannot succeed.

Each child has his or her own individuality. In the light of faith, parents will serve this new life by helping it to stand freely on its own. The range of true freedom within which sons and daughters should be able to thrive is the range of genuine love. Happy are those children who can experience the almighty love that despite their faults watches over them. Happy are those children who have learned from their parents the art of finding life by giving it to others. Happy are those boys and girls who from their youngest age have learned from their parents to love Christ and to heed his call.

Respect for parents reaches out as well to grandparents and to all older people, especially to those who have been abandoned by their families. To love them also means to create conditions that insure their well-being and sense of belonging to the life of the human and Christian community.

What are we doing for the future of the family?

"Honor your father and your mother, that you may have a long life in the land" (Exod 20:12) "and prosperity" (Deut 5:16). This double promise by the Lord shows that happiness belongs to society and to each individual. The long life or vitality of a people depends on the climate that prevails in its families. The health of the whole community and that of the Church depends upon the quality of life that is found in the smallest cell of society and of the Church—the home.

Not all families have the same chances for success. Many suffer different trials (bereavement, prolonged illness, separation, unemployment, etc.). Therefore it is important to develop a sense of community within and among families.

5. You shall not kill: you shall respect human life

"I love life!"

The fifth commandment makes us aware that human life is a gift of God and that we must respect and foster the lives of all human beings.

A person accepts the life that he or she has received only gradually, day by day. In spite of all troubles, the vast majority of people are nonetheless happy to be alive, even when life becomes hard to accept. Still, some people have to reconcile themselves with life in order to be able to fully accept it. It is fair to say that life is a struggle, a struggle with oneself, with others, and with the conditions of life that have been given us. Despite everything, this struggle must not degenerate into a denial of life, whether our own or another's.

God calls us to live forever. This love of life is first of all a love of self. The Lord commands that we love our neighbor *as ourselves.* Our love for our neighbor will be poor indeed if we do not love ourselves. Only the one who loves

one's self and who respects one's self is able to love another with an open and blossoming love.

The gospel casts the value of human life in a new light. God has taken on the human condition, has restored men and women to life, and has healed the sick. Through the new life that he has offered us by giving himself up to death, he has made us children of the Father and brothers and sisters to one another. Ever since humans have peopled the earth, ever since humans have struggled to survive, God has willed for all to have life and have it abundantly, even newly conceived life in a mother's womb. The Christian makes this will of God his or her own. Christians want people to live, and to live well.

"The glory of God is the living person . . ."

This human love implies respect for human life and all that it entails. To live and to live well, people need social recognition and untarnished reputations. They have a right to a moral and a spiritual life and a climate of social and cultural life that allows them to breathe. To achieve this, believers do not limit themselves to a purely individual commitment. They realize that collectively they must influence their environment and spread the word about God's gift of life.

". . . yet the life of each person is to see God" (St. Irenaeus).

Believers are called to witness to their faith by promoting whatever protects *all* human life. There are social structures that slowly kill moral and religious values, and others that slowly secure them. Christians are in community with all human beings whether or not they share in the faith. Wherever men and women dedicate themselves to human rights, and especially to those most deprived, Christians are among them. They are called to mutual respect, collaboration, understanding beyond divisiveness, and to regulate material, moral, and spiritual living conditions within society.

The Christian community acknowledges those who share the ideas of Joseph Cardijn, the Belgian priest who was at the forefront of the Catholic Action movement. The community must work to uphold the dignity of the working person who labors in a just and peaceful world.

Our life proceeds from *God's* hands and we should take care of it. Health is a marvelous thing. It requires cleanliness, exercise, appropriate rest, and medical care. Abuse of alcohol, tobacco, or drugs can poison the body. To be in good health and to maintain it is a gift to ourselves and to those around us: our spouses, our children, and our par-

Taking care of oneself

ents. In all this the Christian lives out love for self and for others.

The cult of the body or the cultivation of human qualities?

Advertising depicts images of the ideal body and of exaggerated well-being that are unrealistic. The truth is that a man or a woman must accept what he or she actually is, with the body that he or she has. Despite the advertising dream of eternal youth, we grow older. It is not easy to age serenely and to accept dying. Nevertheless, good things can happen between healthy people and those less healthy. Friendship and warm relations make life human. Loneliness can age a person more than the passing of years.

Is human life an absolute?

The promise of the resurrection gives a Christian courage in the face of the degenerative process, since "our inner self is being renewed day by day," even though our body is being destroyed at the same time (2 Cor 4:16), says St. Paul, who wore himself out in apostolic toil.

Christians, while loving life, do not idolize their own lives: they know they are called to use life, as they received it, for the love of their brothers and sisters, for "there is no greater love than when a man gives his life for his friends," as Jesus said.

Giving and respecting one's life

Jesus died *for us.* There are men and women in this world who die as martyrs in order to give witness to the gospel or to defend their human dignity or the dignity of others. This is beautiful and good.

Others decide to finish themselves off. For them, life is no longer worth the trouble. The precept, "You shall not kill," is addressed first of all to ourselves: "You shall not kill yourself." In the eyes of faith, every human life is worth the pain of living, even if psychologically or physically diminished. To be sure, a Christian does not make a cult out of suffering, and whatever physicians can do to allay the sufferings of illnesses is a benefit for humankind.

Facing death, a Christian may accept his or her state of physical destitution and may decline intensive therapy: "Father, into your hands I commend my life." Nevertheless, one may not willfully seek to bring about one's own death. Euthanasia is an attack upon a human life, whether one's own or another's, and it is incompatible with Christian faith.

In our society there are some people, even very young ones, who despair of life and commit suicide. To combat suicide, it is first of all necessary to recognize reasons for living—

182

Christian reasons for living! The Church condemns suicide as it does euthanasia. The same holds true for abortion. Every Christian and every human being should conscientiously strive to provide remedies to combat the psychological, familial, economic, or social circumstances that can lead human beings to do away with themselves, or lead a mother or a couple to destroy a child in the womb. The Church appeals to everyone's conscience and wants to give witness to Christian hope even at the very core of suffering.

"Get out of my way!": rivalries and rage

It may be that our lack of respect for life has its source in our rivalries, our anxieties, and our rage. Jesus tells us not to let envy and wrath gnaw away at our hearts. We ought not to provoke our neighbors or allow ourselves to be provoked by them. The Lord invites us to reconciliation with our neighbor whenever there is trouble between us and before we address God in prayer (Matt 5:21-26).

Jesus invites us to adopt the gospel attitude of encouragement. For this, he gives us the Golden Rule: "Do to others whatever you would have them do to you" (Matt 7:12).

The escalation of violence, and reconciliation

In following Jesus, the Christian says "no" to violence and to reprisals that answer violence with greater violence. Surrounded by hate, he or she sees the need to pardon according to Jesus' example. Hanging from the cross, the Lord prayed for his enemies: "Father, forgive them, they know not what they do" (Luke 23:34). He gave us this power to forgive by giving us his Spirit. This is why Stephen, the first Christian martyr, while filled with the Holy Spirit, said "Lord, do not hold this sin against them" (Acts 7:60).

Should a Christian accept whatever happens? War and the death penalty?

We can also create a climate of fear toward other nations that leads to increasing defense armament and engenders a mistrust that prevents real negotiation. Every person, every group, every nation has the right to defend its existence and its legitimate interests, both material and spiritual. It can happen that this legitimate defense has to be carried out through weapons, but war should be only the last resort. Humanity has the duty to negotiate peace. To negotiate means to relinquish a *part* of what one thinks one can win by force; if both parties to a conflict demand *all* that they want, war is inevitable.

A Christian must be a person of peace who, in all circumstances, urges people to build a more just world through dialogue and negotiation. According to the recommendation of the Second Vatican Council, we are called "to tackle . . . this task of supreme love for man which is the building up of a lasting peace" (*Gaudium et Spes* 82,2). It is necessary to pray unceasingly to God to give us this energy because it is the work of grace that inclines the heart. Only God can grant us the ultimate peace. It is Christ crucified who has done this by destroying all hate.

The waning of popular support for the death penalty represents progress for humanity. The Church holds that every person, however guilty, has the right to a fair trial and that every prisoner has the right to humane conditions. Human life, even that of a murderer, is sacred. There are, however, some limited cases that still call for the death penalty in order to remove an evil from society and thus protect its members. Every society, however, should move to create social and moral conditions where such punishment is no longer appropriate.

Violence often seeks to justify itself through fear. This is especially true in our fear of foreigners. Foreigners and other strangers make us feel uncomfortable because their cultural and religious behavior is different from ours. Yet, whatever their differences, Christians should treat every stranger as a brother or sister, a child of God like themselves.

Every human being is profoundly vulnerable. To try to destroy someone psychologically, to make another's life unlivable, or to incite someone to sin is incompatible with faith in him who died so that human beings could live, and live in his Life. The gospel teaches us how Jesus identifies himself with the person who is hungry and thirsty, with the stranger, the sick person, and the prisoner: "Whatever you did for one of these least brothers of mine, you did for me" (Matt 25:40).

Indifference "kills" those who suffer, and saps the courage of those who struggle for their brothers and sisters in our society, and in Third- and Fourth-World countries. This is why the Christian community has the duty to share materially, morally, and spiritually in this effort lest we injure our own Christian vitality.

Be careful of what you do to these little ones!

6. You shall not commit adultery; your love shall remain faithful

"Men and women . . ." The sixth commandment concerns love and sexuality. "God created man in his image; in the divine image he created him; male and female he created them" (Gen 1:27).

God has entrusted all of creation to humanity, that is, to man and to woman, so that they might jointly care for it and humanize it. Woman draws man out of his isolation in building the world, and vice-versa. The fact that we are men and women is a source of joy in all spheres of life. Everywhere we are surprised at discovering a touch of the masculine or the feminine in our environment. Thus from birth a child experiences the pleasure of being loved in turn by a mother and a father, by men and women who take pleasure in the child's pleasure. From the cradle the child learns to be a "man" or a "woman," for our sexuality is a basic component of our personality; it is a mode of existing, of making oneself known, of communicating with others, of feeling, of expressing, and of living human love. While similar, we are also *different*. What a joy it is sometimes to see our universe through the eyes of the opposite sex!

What is chastity? The Church attaches particular importance to teaching about human love that is experienced sexually. It takes care to see that human beings learn healthy control of their sexuality, calling upon each person to practice chastity in both celibacy and in marriage. Spouses should live out their relationship as husband and wife by being attentive to their partner's different approach to life. They should understand that joy in loving implies some renunciation. Pleasure in marriage is fleeting without a couple's mutual respect for one another. This respect also carries over into childbearing, because giving birth to a child means that everything in the marriage is conducive to welcoming a new member into the family and into the human community.

Adultery What we are about to say shows how respectful Christians are about human sexuality, recognizing it as a gift from God. Man and woman participate in the creative love of God, not only as individual persons but also as a couple. The body, as sexual instrument, acts to fulfill the human desire to unite with the opposite sex. The Christian couple is aware of the Holy Spirit's role in their marriage. Thus they live out their vocation in the Church through the grace of the sacrament of marriage. "You shall not commit adultery" means that you shall respect the promise you gave in church to your vocation as a couple, and you will respect your partner who has also made a promise to you.

Adultery, or extramarital relations, cannot be accurately evaluated from the standpoint of just one person. It also involves the wronged spouse, as well as the person with whom one commits adultery, that person's own spouse, if any, and sometimes the children on either side. Serious conjugal infidelity can also occur without actual sexual relations.

In the view of the gospel, he or she who is unfaithful to his or her spouse, in actions or intentions, is unfaithful to God's Church and to the Spirit who makes the Church one body; he or she damages the Church and society.

In looking at the results of adultery, we usually find that the separated spouse, especially the innocent spouse, suffers loneliness and other familial and social hardships. The ecclesial community must concern itself with specific help to

Divorce

support that person's faith. Divorced people who sometimes heroically refuse to remarry give faithful and courageous witness to the indissolubility of their Christian marriage. They are invited to renew the power of this witness by receiving the sacraments frequently. Divorced people who are remarried in civil ceremonies are invited to listen to the Word of God, to attend the Eucharistic celebration, and to persevere in prayer to implore the grace of God day after day. Even if the Church cannot absolve them or admit them to Eucharistic communion, it continues to care about them. The Christian community is called not to judge them but to search for ways that allow divorced and remarried people to be with God and their brethren even though the Church remains completely on the side of permanent marriage.

Sanctification of the home

The demands of Christian family life require the sanctification of the home. This is accomplished on a day-by-day basis. The human and spiritual journey of the spouses calls for an enlightened conscience about sin in all its forms, as well as a shared commitment, maturely discussed, to observe the law of the Lord. Spouses are aided here by the grace of the Eucharist and by the sacrament of reconciliation, which involves practicing mutual forgiveness. This journey must be accompanied by a life of prayer. Each spouse should take an active role, not leaving all initiative up to the other. The family setting remains the appropriate place for teaching youths about chastity. This gradual family education aims at the all-around development of young people, who should be given the chance to see, by their parents' life of prayer, that adults are as unprotected and vulnerable as they.

Around the cradle the spouses discover their new roles of mother and father, "servants" of the great mystery of life (*Gaudium et Spes,* 50, 1). The arrival of a child makes the union of a man and a woman into a true family. In a way, the child establishes the home. And it will be welcomed all the more if parents fully and mutually accept each other from the depths of their being. To give life to a child does not mean that it will sometimes be "your" child or "my" child. The child should be "ours," desired and accepted for just what it is. A child is not merely the product of a couple's ability to reproduce, but of the *relationship* of the parents-to-be with the child about to be born. This new relationship should deepen the loving relationship between the spouses.

To speak of regulating births in general terms of contraception and birth control, without reference to the dimension we are about to describe, is to neglect the fact that a child is not an object, but rather a person and a gift from God. In talking about birth control, Christians must take into full consideration the union of the spouses, the good of the children already born, and the good of any child awaiting birth in the womb.

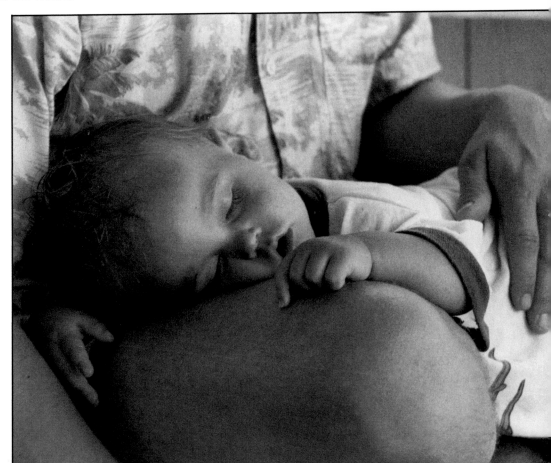

Birth control

The Christian community ought to give encouragement to parents who accept their child by trusting in the love of God, a love that alone is stronger than all societal fears. This is why the Church vigorously points out what is at stake regarding the regulation of births from a human and spiritual perspective. It strives to explain to Christians that only natural family planning methods best respect the demands of responsible parenthood: they maintain respect for the nature of the conjugal act, acceptance of a dialogue between spouses, and for mutual respect for one another and parental responsibility.

In contrast, the Church cannot accept artificial methods of contraception, which tend to undervalue the human and spiritual character of conjugal love. Thus Christians are faced with their responsibilities: they are called to follow the direction of their blossoming conjugal life and to fully assume their parental vocation.

Education in chastity

The Second Vatican Council asks that young people be given the benefit of a sexual education that is both positive and prudent, at a level appropriate to their stage of growth. Our body is the first message that God gives us. As a sexual instrument, it expresses the human vocation to mutuality, namely, the love of a husband for his wife and of a wife for her husband. Christian education in a healthy, ordered sexuality needs to be considered in the context of gospel values. Christian parents should be the first to reveal to their children and adolescents the design of the human person that characterizes their bodies. They are the ones who by example will teach the kind of self-esteem and modesty that should accompany a young person's gradual discovery of his or her body. Beyond providing mere cognitive information, Christian parents must also strive to develop willpower in their children and teach them how to assess their feelings and emotions by encouraging trust in God.

An authentic education will lead to self-mastery, to consistency in moral choices, and to strength of character. One delicate problem that arises in one's sexual development is that of autoeroticism. Christian morality considers masturbation to be a selfish act, especially in an adult, since sexuality as willed by God is oriented not toward oneself but toward another, toward the mutual desire of the spouses for each other and their desire for a child.

Autoeroticism

While keeping in mind the objective gravity of masturbation, we should be cautious in judging a person's actual responsibility in the matter. One needs to feel a welcome part of a caring community in order to be freed of the desire to withdraw into oneself. Care must be taken to neither dramatize masturbation nor trivialize it.

"You must know that your body is a temple of the Holy Spirit."

Sometimes in a young person or in an adult the habit of autoeroticism results from a lack of spiritual motivation and from a pagan concept of the body. In the light of faith the body is the "temple of the holy Spirit" (1 Cor 6:19). To help oneself live by this faith, it is important to lead a healthy life, to nourish one's spiritual life in prayer and the sacraments, and to develop an attentiveness toward others that engages all of one's person.

Is all sexual love moral?

It is possible that a Christian must deal with another problem, namely, homosexuality. Homosexual *tendencies* do not constitute an object for moral judgment. It is homosexual *genital acts* that are forbidden. Indeed, such acts lack an essential and indispensable dimension for moral justification. Only the heterosexual dimension respects the conjugal act in its double dimension of union and procreation.

Giving respect means neither excluding nor permitting everything.

Like adultery—indeed like all serious sins—sinful homosexual behavior precludes a good relationship with God, with one's family, and with society. Despite the stricture of objective morality, the guilt of homosexual acts needs to be judged with charity and prudence. Accepting homosexuals with understanding implies that they will not be turned away from the Church community but rather supported as they endeavor to live in accord with the teaching of Christ and the Church.

The engagement period for fiancés is most important. It allows the couple time to learn as much as possible about each other and prepares them for lifelong fidelity to the forthcoming sacred vow of marriage. It remains, however, a time to refrain from conjugal relations because, for the baptized, the conjugal act of sexual intercourse is reserved solely for the married state, since it symbolizes the unbreakable union of Christ and the Church.

Cohabitation, in which the couple live together with the understanding that nothing is definite, is not preparation for marriage. It is *already* a life in common but without either the commitment of one to another or public commitment before the community. This kind of life does not prepare one for ultimate faithfulness. On the contrary, it signifies a rejection, at least temporarily, of the irreversible bond through which Christian spouses publicly commit themselves to one another with the grace of God before society and the Church.

True preparation for marriage involves patience. Love provides self-mastery and upholds mutual respect. Patience and sensitivity are qualities that are vital for mutual fidelity. Sexual relations make up part of the rich language of human love. If premature, they can jeopardize the complete flowering of this love. Continence, too, is part of this language of love and is a form of expression that is as important during the engagement as during the marriage.

Can love do without prohibitions in order to grow?

Many men and women do not marry, through circumstance, by choice, vocation, or by consecration. For celibates, Christian chastity consists of living their sexuality in healthy continence as a sign of the strong union between Christ and his Church. The faithfulness of spouses finds support in the faithfulness of celibates who remain in waiting, body and soul, for the new world—that of the resurrection, when marrying will no longer exist.

Living out chastity in celibacy

Where there is esteem for marriage, there is also esteem for celibacy and consecrated virginity. Where human sexuality is considered a great gift of the Creator, the renunciation of it for the sake of the Kingdom has its full meaning.

7. You shall not enslave or exploit a human being; you shall safeguard each person's freedom and dignity

You shall not steal.

The seventh commandment prohibits stealing, but it stands for much more. In the Bible, this prohibition deals not only with stealing in general but primarily of the theft of men, women, and children who were seized in the course of raids and reduced to slavery. Today this commandment still stands in all its gravity: it covers the exploitation of a human being by another and addresses the issue of dishonesty.

God wants us to be free.

Human beings have been created in God's image and likeness: they are not objects. They have been freed from slavery and redeemed from the captivity of sin. In all ages, however, they have been seized upon, bought and sold . . . Jesus himself was sold and condemned to a slave's death. He took upon himself all the sufferings of the innocents who even today are used for political or economic purposes or to gratify a sexual, mercenary, or violent passion: the taking of hostages; torture and unwarranted confinement in psychiatric wards; "disappearances" by the thousands under dictatorial regimes; "cheap" labor imported from other countries or exploited on site; populations crowded onto frontiers, chased from their lands, bought along with their lands, or penned into vast ghettos; oppression of men, women, and children to be exploited in mines, quarries, plantations, drug factories, and trafficking; prostitution of adults and children; commerce in embryos, "wombs for rent." . . .

The exploitation of human beings *by* human beings constitutes, throughout the world, its own form of commerce and industry. It plays a major role in the basic structure of the world economy and has its repercussions in every country. We must expose it, become aware of it, and act upon its causes and its consequences. This responsibility places us at the core of the Christian vocation. Daily newspapers and television show us the poor Lazarus of the parable (Luke 16:19-31) lying at our feet, on the threshold of the door of the rich people that we are. He challenges us to dress his terrible wounds.

Educating oneself into solidarity

The Church's social doctrine is based on the dignity of the human person. A young person or a laborer is worth more than all the gold in the world. Many are ready to acknowledge this, but few draw practical conclusions from it. Faced with such a great number of hungry people in the world, the Second Vatican Council insists that all people and authorities recall this saying from the Fathers of the Church: "Give to the one who is dying of hunger, for if you have not given him something to eat, you have killed him." The Council insists that all people, to the extent that they can, truly share their possessions. This sharing should enable individuals and nations to obtain the means to help and develop themselves (*Gaudium et Spes* 69, 1). It is not enough to give; one must give knowingly, as a way of becoming more human and more free.

According to the Catholic concept of work, human beings not only share in the creative work of God; through offering their work to God, they are also associated with the redemptive work of Jesus Christ, who endowed work with eminent dignity by working in Nazareth with his hands for the greater part of his life. Work brings people together and makes them freer, both morally and physically.

The human vocation to work

We are confronted with a disconcerting and unjust worldwide phenomenon. In places where natural resources remain unused, millions of men and women are either unemployed or remain underemployed, and they die of hunger. Millions of others are exploited and die of exhaustion. The responsibilities of industrialized countries and of leadership echelons in developing countries are important. The search for adequate remedies is urgent.

The task of making the world more human falls upon all humanity; no one can be excluded. Every person, whatever his or her culture, religion, or race, should be able to find a place that can be called "home." Work is a sacred right of every person.

The right of everyone to work is sacred.

Unemployment is an injustice that demoralizes everyone, especially young people. It deprives people of the important means to achieve a personal balance and the joy of feeling themselves to be useful coworkers in building the city; it removes from them the possibility of exercising their responsibilities.

The obligation to compensate the unemployed stems directly from the right, common to all people, to have access to the necessities of life and to be able to work. A kinship between an employed person and one who is unfairly deprived of work is fundamental. It is not the unemployed who should be ashamed at not having work but rather the human community for not finding any to offer them.

The production of goods involves women as well as men. Women play a specific role in this and, accordingly, have the right to work. It is necesary to take into account their qualities as women, however, without giving rise to discrimination. Work in the home should be as recognized and respected as any other.

Immigrant workers should have the same social rights and advantages as national citizens. They must not be discriminated against, racially or otherwise. The Christian sees every person as a brother or sister, and every person has a right to the freedom that we all cherish in our hearts.

Likewise, people with disabilities must not be excluded from the workplace. The humanization of our society demands that tasks within their capabilities be made available to them. A society that does not dutifully accept this is guilty of discrimination against its weaker and less healthy members.

Various injustices prevent many families from enjoying their fundamental family rights. Unemployment demoralizes spouses and children. It is not just a social drama. It is a moral drama as well.

What to do? Moving from ideas to concrete action.

As for redistributing the work available, many initiatives have been suggested, some more significant than others: doing away with overtime hours and second jobs; shortening work hours wherever possible; creating useful jobs in fields that until now have been neglected; drafting worthwhile alternative laws; part-time work; campaigning against abuses; easing access to independent professions; better coordinating professional work, managerial tasks, and social commitment.

Another criterion for judging the justice of a socio-economic system is that of the just salary. If compensation for work is not enough, society should reexamine its organizational bases of work. To be just, society must be constantly attentive to its members' real-life situations. A salary level that permits heads of households to handle all their responsibilities is a primary consideration in evaluating a just salary.

Mothers of families have the right to family allowances so they can raise their children and not have to work outside the home.

Besides a just salary, medical assistance for workers should be financially guaranteed. In the event of an accident in the workplace, the worker has a right to be compensated for injuries. In general, all social, legal, or contractual arrangements involve a real moral obligation for the contracting parties.

In a society in which we all have the problem of saving for the future, some kind of social security system is obviously necessary, not only as an individual right but for social stability.

All social groups have the right to form unions in order to defend their vital interests and to appoint spokespersons who can relate their concerns to other qualified partners in society. It goes without saying that their activity may involve taking positions that affect the political sector. These groups must nonetheless guard against unilaterally defending their particular interests and privileges to the exclusion of political action.

Defense of the interests of different social groups, and social harmony

The particular vocation of lay Christians is to act as a leaven in the world. They are called to dialogue and to collaborate with people of diverse persuasions on the political, economic, and social level, in order to protect the interests of the greatest number of people, especially those most deprived.

The Church does not have a solution for every problem

When the Church so clearly expresses this duty of the Christian community, it is not displacing experts in economics or politics. Nor does it pretend to have the solution to every single problem; but it *does* appeal to consciences. It vigorously calls Christians to action, particularly those who think that "nothing can be done about it."

In our country, as in the Third World, hundreds of thousands of people, generation after generation, are excluded from sharing in our prosperity. Socially maladapted, they make up what is called the Fourth World. There are various reaons that contribute to their living conditions: insufficient income, health problems, illiteracy, lack of skills, and wretched housing. Men and women of the Fourth World are not beyond help; experience shows us that they are capable of getting on their feet. If our attention, help, and

support are aimed at their human development, we can help them to find their way in our labyrinth of legality, and we can inform them about their rights, of which they are ignorant.

Struggling against poverty

We sometimes hear someone say, "As long as there are children dying of hunger, I will not be able to eat in peace!" Or again, "When you see that kind of misery, you think you've gotten your own happiness by stealing." Does the gospel make us guilt-ridden? There is a level of well-being that we can receive or acquire fairly. This does not mean that happiness is achieved by stealing, or that all of life should be burdened with a false feeling of guilt. Christians are called to give thanks for their happiness and to share it. They do have responsibilities, but these have their limits. No one is bound to do the impossible. Each one's responsibility is limited to what is morally obligatory and to what is his or her own capability.

Within the context of real solidarity, attitudes must change. How can work be redistributed if everybody feels he or she has the right to consume without limit? Yet it is entirely possible if everyone, at his or her level, is content with having less. The Christian finds in Jesus' message reasons for conversion:

"Thus will it be for the one who stores up treasure for himself but is not rich in what matters to God. . . . For life is more than food and the body more than clothing. . . . Instead, seek his kingdom, and these other things will be given you besides" (Luke 12:21, 23, 31).

Such campaigns as the Campaign for Human Development, Bread for the World, and Oxfam International are the kinds of programs that impel us to share our wealth. It matters little that this makes us slightly "poorer," with a less expensive automobile, a lower degree of comfort, a shorter trip, or a more restrained diet. "It is more blessed to give than to receive" (Acts 20:35).

Everyone knows that in our culture time is money. The Christian community gives encouragement to those young people and adults who, in our country and in the Third World, give their time freely for the benefit of those most in need. Often receiving more in return from their brothers and sisters than they give, they struggle against the poverty in their hearts. Some have no qualms about giving several years' service or even their entire lifetimes, sacrificing their comfort and careers. Through their generosity and determination they spontaneously create around themselves networks of awakened consciences and a spirit of community that prove to be potent yeast within the dough.

"If someone who has worldly means sees a brother in need and refuses him compassion, how can the love of God remain in him?" (1 John 3:17). Personal generosity in no way excuses Christians from working with their brethren for the transformation of unjust structures in society: it is a door open to the unlimited power of the Holy Spirit, the source of every liberating action.

A utopia . . .

The Book of the Acts of the Apostles describes the first Christian community as a model for us: "All who believed were together and had all things in common; they would sell their property and possessions and divide them among all according to each one's need. . . . There was no needy person among them" (Acts 2:44-45; 4:34). In this text is a call of which we find a resonant echo in certain Christian communities of religious and of others: they are signs of the world to come. Yet each baptized person is called to share in the prophetic mission of the Church. When one shares with the poverty-stricken, he or she collaborates in the future as willed by God, and demonstrates that love is possible among all people.

. . . that is quite realistic!

How is this aspect of justice manifested concretely today? The community's responsibilities should be equitably shared according to each person's means. Taxes are one of the means for redistributing wealth and should be honestly paid. It is always dishonest to contribute to weakening a country's economy for one's own profit by investing money abroad. The same can be said for using social movements for purposes other than social justice. Abuses of bad management, squandering of church or state property, vandalism in public places, and cheating on public transportation have their worst effects on the disadvantaged.

Cultivating honesty

All around us honesty and respect for one another are in decline: cheating on examinations and on documents of all kinds; thefts of cars, bicycles, handbags; shoplifting, armed robbery . . . To end this plague we must create a wholesome attitude in a wholesome environment.

The cultivation of honesty is essential for showing forth the justice of God.

8. Your witness shall be true; speak well of your neighbor

The eighth commandment seeks to root out from the human heart lying and unkindness that is spread by word of mouth. It brings us into the realm of truth at a depth where "kindness and truth shall meet" (Ps 85:11) and where the disciple becomes like his master, the "faithful and true witness" (Rev 3:14).

What is truth?

Truth is something not easily defined. It is more than exposing what is real, i.e., "reality" in its philosophical sense. The Bible tells us that truth is trust, a kind of rock-solid support that a person can lean on. Jesus is the Truth because we are able to count on him. He is the true way and the true life. This is the truth that is required of Christians. It is not, then, a matter of knowing what we are going to do with "reality," whether we expose it, but rather of knowing how we are going to treat our neighbors and support them just as God supports them!

Whom can the condemned person depend upon?

"You shall not bear false witness against your neighbor": this biblical commandment was applied above all to witnessing for justice. The very fate of Hebrew people often depended on good or bad witness. Accused persons had to prove their innocence. If two persons testified against the accused, the case was closed. Everything depended on witnesses: honor, freedom, life. This is why punishment was so severe for bearing false witness: one was punished by receiving the same penalty appropriate to the fault they had accused their neighbor of. Even today, false witness is an especially serious fault. It makes a mockery of justice and plays games with the lives of people and their families.

Haven't we killed Truth?

The danger of being judged in a hasty, disrespectful, or anonymous way is always present. Everywhere in the world people are condemned for various actions with or without a trial. Justice is blind when it superficially judges a verdict on "hearsay" (Isa 11:3). Wasn't Jesus condemned to death on the basis of false testimonies—he who is Truth?

What do they say about me?

The Spirit the Lord has given us is the source of truth and courage. The world needs witnesses who do justice to human truth, and this need is not confined to the courts. Our whole life is a call to give honest witness to one another. Nowadays, people are extremely sensitive to the good or harm that a person can bring about. They want to

200

find someone who knows and understands them, who sees not only their weaknesses but also their strengths. Who is the witness who will respectfully defend me?

Should we not, more than ever, be careful about what we say or do not say? The gift of language is the most marvelous thing God has given us. It reveals us to one another; it enables us to make ourselves deeply understood, yet it can also become a murderous tool. The Apostle James says, "Consider how small a fire can set a huge forest ablaze. The tongue is also a fire . . . but no human being can tame the tongue. With it we bless the Lord and Father, and with it we curse human beings who are made in the likeness of God" (James 3:5-6, 8, 9). Within several minutes we can reduce the name and reputation of another to ashes. How many years does it take for the forest to become green again? This admonition applies to slander (broadcasting a real evil) and even more to calumny (falsely imputing evil). It applies to the one who spreads the evil report and also to the one who encourages the first by lending an ear to the malicious word. Lying, prejudices, slander, and calumny are all the more serious when they wound a neighbor and destroy personal trust. They menace the Church's unity by introducing mistrust among its members.

Like a forest fire!

Each of our words takes the side either of trustworthiness or of lying. It is through our words and our deeds that we prove we are brothers and sisters and that we are near to those of whom we speak. Paul says, "Therefore, putting away falsehood, speak the truth, each one to his neighbor, for we are members one of another" (Eph 4:25). Being members means being close. Lying belongs to the believer's pre-Christian period. By lying, one demonstrates that his or her conversion is not complete. To tell the truth, to speak well of one's neighbor and to say it publicly, to seek to make up for telling bad things about another, and to set a good example by so doing is to build up the Christian community where love abounds.

Let our words bring us closer to one another.

The eighth commandment does not merely demand telling the truth; it is still necessary to tell it without maligning our neighbor. Indeed, there is no knife more cutting than the truth. The more overpowering the truth, the more lethal it can be. Christians who state the truth to their brethren should also be the first to help them live within it.

Learning to tell the truth

To "tell it like it is" about someone else is really to humiliate that other person. The truth told by a kind heart is the

only truth. Indeed, telling the truth with love or with malice are two entirely different things. I ought not to utter the truth that kills or that leads another person into despair. I am *not* my neighbor's judge.

To learn to tell the truth to oneself is to learn to love oneself under the ever-loving gaze of God. When Peter betrayed his master, Jesus turned toward him and . . . Peter wept. When Judas betrayed Jesus, he saw what he had done with chilling clarity and plunged into despair: he hanged himself! When, in a moment of truth and moved by grace we acknowledge our sin, we know that the Spirit of truth who works within us is already acting to reconcile us with God; it is he who sustains us. "Father, I have done what is evil in your sight!" Here lucidity brings one to the unshakeable love of the Father. Far from languishing in the shadows, "whoever lives the truth comes to the light" (John 3:21) because he has received the Father's love.

Silence also speaks. In the search for love and truth, silence is a language. It can be a weakness. It is often a power. At times it requires heroism. Keeping secrets contributes to mutual trust. Every individual has a right to discretion in areas belonging to his or her private life. One who through professional activity (such as a physician) gains access to people's private lives is bound to professional secrecy. A priest may not tell what he learns in confession to anyone, even with the penitent's permission. In order for a confessor to be able even to use the confessed information where it might be necessary or because the penitent desires it, it is necessary for the penitent to repeat, outside of confession, the information he

202

wants to communicate. Indeed, the advantage of the sacrament requires that the faithful be able to place total trust in the priest while asking for the pardon of God and his Church. This trust is based on the absolute secrecy the priest is bound to observe.

One must never lie. But what is lying? It means to impair relationships among people by words or behavior that destroy trust. One may never lie because every human being has the right to trust another. To conceal the truth from people, partially or totally, because the truth would be too heavy for them to bear, is not to lie to them but to spare them. What matters primarily is that one must act with equal concern for the welfare of the other person and for the relationship of trust.

May one "lie" under certain circumstances?

To withhold facts from someone who has no right to know them is not lying. The Christian principle is twofold: one may tell the truth only to someone who has the right to know it and the strength to bear it; and one may tell the truth to another only in a way that the other can bear it.

It is not a lie to utter a counter-truth in order to protect someone morally or physically: "No, my father is not a drunkard; no, no one is hiding here . . ." To keep a confidence, one can evade a question and keep quiet or pull a veil over what one knows or soften a truth that is too hard for someone, yet still encourage the person by telling him or her things that are partially true: "I've met people who greatly appreciate what you are doing."

To remain quiet or to soften the truth is not something to be done lightly! To open oneself to the truth is a constant demand. There are circumstances when one should be able to admit certain truths without equivocation or to inform other people about them. We will always need prophets who dare to proclaim the truth.

Can one be obliged to say what one knows?

It is sometimes necessary for the good of everyone to reveal a hidden evil to competent persons. This has nothing to do with a desire for sensationalism or with unsavory revelations in which one can take easy and smug satisfaction ("I thank you, Lord, that I am not like those people"). This is why the press and the information media have a positive role to play for the public good, by being vigilant and informing audiences and readers with honesty. Truth proceeds from the Spirit of the Lord and not from the spirit of Evil One.

There are men and women who are willing to die for the truth, which is admirable, and who struggle to insure that the cloak of silence that weighs heavily upon their tortured brethren not be a cloak of deceit or indifference.

We must first of all affirm our social unity: it is not enough to say that we are all children of the same Father. We must make it believable.

Witnessing through deeds does not excuse us from witnessing through words. To be a Christian *in truth* means to give witness to the faith that enlivens us. Every silence undermines the community's witness. People may deny their faith either because they are afraid of what others might say or think, or they might be ashamed of Christ. On the other hand, the Christian community is nourished by the witness of those who have given their lives in publicly confessing their faith for the love of their brothers and sisters. The Church calls them martyrs, i.e., witnesses.

The Evil One is always at work. Slothful ignorance and closed minds distort the meaning of the gospel and the Church's teaching. We should turn from this through prayer and diligent discipline of conscience. To speak and be convinced of the truth of faith is to understand with a poor person's heart:

"If you remain in my word,
you will truly be my disciples,
and you will know the truth,
and the truth will set you free" (John 8:31-32).

9. You shall remain pure in all thoughts and desires

For catechetical reasons, the Church has made two commandments out of the tenth biblical one: "You shall not covet your neighbor's house. You shall not covet your neighbor's wife . . . nor anything that belongs to him" (cf. Exod 20:17). In the Catholic and Lutheran traditions, the ninth commandment concerns the wrongful desire that leads to adultery; the tenth commandment is about the desire to have something that belongs to another.

What difference is there between desiring and coveting?

Humans are creatures with desires, and therein lies their nobility. Desire opens a person's heart to someone else: to desire to live, comfort, to succeed, love, and be loved—what is more beautiful? Covetousness, however, means to

204

take everything only for oneself and to add to one's possessions to the point of disdain for God and neighbor.

In the Old Testament, "to covet" is a very realistic term that encompasses not only the thought but also whatever leads to the act, which consists of scheming to accomplish one's purposes. To covet is to act.

In the New Testament, Jesus denounces the hypocrisy of those who honor God only with their lips and not with their hearts (Matt 15:6-8). He demands integrity from a person in word and deed. Everything comes from the heart, truth as well as lying. Catholic tradition speaks here of "purity of heart." This embraces all the commandments: "For from the heart come evil thoughts, murder, adultery, unchastity, theft, false witness, blasphemy" (Matt 15:19-20). Coveting is an intention that, even if it does not end in action, is already malicious. This is why Jesus is so radical. "Everyone who looks at a woman with lust has already committed adultery with her in his heart" (Matt 5:28). Even before we act, antisocial sins erupt in the heart. Proceeding from an evil heart, they reveal its wickedness.

At the beginning of the Sermon on the Mount, Jesus says, "Happy the pure in heart" (Matt 5:8, JB). What does this mean? The first meaning of *pure* is "genuine," in the sense of pure wine or pure gold. Thus, the psalmist can say, "he whose hands are clean, whose heart is pure, whose soul does not pay homage to worthless things and who never swears to a lie . . ." (Ps 24:4, JB). The word *pure* also evokes "transparency." When the glass is pure, it lets light through it. "Happy the pure in heart: they shall see God" (Matt 5:8, JB). "If your eye is sound, your whole body will be filled with light" (Matt 6:22 JB). Those who love God with their whole heart, with their whole soul, and with their whole mind, see clearly by the love they bring to their neighbor. *Pure* can also mean "of only one piece." Jesus demands that we be "perfect" or "upright." Our will to do well ought to be "upright," without a mixture of good and evil.

For Jesus, the Ten Commandments are summed up in one alone: love God and neighbor. Thus those who love God are not steeped in themselves: their love for neighbor gradually becomes real. They do not envy their neighbors but rather love them. A pure heart loves another as oneself, through the very love of God. Pure hearts are "happy." They will see God, since they love him without any malice filtering away the love of God in them.

The ninth commandment pays particular attention to the area of love and sexuality. It is not mainly a question of sexuality in itself, but of the exercise of sexuality in relation to another. Adultery is an injustice because it wrongs the neighbor. This is easily seen if we remember the unity given morality by the single commandment to love God and neighbor. One who lusts after the wife or the husband of a neighbor cannot pretend that he or she truly loves God, for that love of neighbor has become hypocritical. If a person puts into action what he or she fantasizes, that person will destroy the happiness of a couple or of a family.

Hasn't all this been said already? The meaning of the sixth commandment is better understood by the Christian meaning of the ninth. Here the evil is considered in its root form: the covetousness that surges from a wicked heart, whose selfishness is harmful to others.

It is not a question of simply having "impure thoughts" with respect to sexuality, or of enjoying them, but of wrongfully desiring someone else's wife or husband, and of entertain-

206

ing this desire. What darkens the picture is the maliciousness of the situation, one that destroys love.

According to gospel principles concerning moral conscience, the meaning of covetousness is extended to all other types of fornication envisioned by the sixth commandment: prostitution, homosexuality, pederasty, autoeroticism . . . . The bad thoughts or desires that spontaneously arise in our minds are not sins. But to entertain or to seek to enjoy them belongs to the works of darkness: it is sinful because it stains the heart that freely consents to it.

"If we say, 'We have fellowship with him,'
while we continue to walk in darkness,
we lie and do not act in truth.
But if we walk in the light
as he is in the light,
then we have fellowship with one another,
and the blood of his Son Jesus cleanses us from all sin"
(1 John 1:6-7).

Today's climate of eroticism is a provocation for everybody, but especially for children and young people who seek to keep a "pure heart," a heart that truly loves.

"Nothing can be done about it; things are not what they used to be!"

The ninth commandment is not limited solely to the covetousness lurking within us. It is also addressed to scandal, i.e., anything we might do to arouse covetousness in others; every act that, directly or indirectly, sows the seed of sinful scheming in the heart of another person. We refer here to the field of education, to the entertainment and advertising industries, to pornography, and to anything that contributes to moral corruption (see Matt 18:6-7).

Is it enough to stay away from "dirty shows" and bad company? The human heart is good, but it is deeply wounded by sin. It is easily seduced by evil. Purity of heart is not within reach of the person who trusts only in him- or herself; it must be asked for in daily prayer. The Christian should have faith in the grace of baptism that has made him or her a "new person" in whom the Holy Spirit dwells.

Love is inventive and creative. All the resources offered by art, entertainment, films, radio and television, meeting places, and recreation facilities can be used to foster the language of genuine love.

Urged on by love for others, Christians, as far as possible, should take an active and creative role in developing forms of culture, leisure, and relaxation that contribute to their well-being. The ninth commandment also appeals to the Christian community to support artists who for the love of humanity focus our attention on the beauty of God's creation. We should encourage other artists to do the same.

10. Look upon your neighbor without coveting his or her goods; see, rather, what you can share with your neighbor

Compared with the ninth, the tenth commandment reveals the human heart from a further perspective. Like sexual covetousness, covetousness over someone else's material possessions is another inner weakness from which Christ has come to free us.

We all seem to want things that we do not yet have. It is fine that we aspire to a worthwhile occupation, a pleasant home . . . yet we can also be "owned" by things we possess or want to possess to the point where we disregard the love of God and of our sisters and brothers. The desire to possess can hold tyrannical sway over ourselves and others. It is not that money is an evil; it is the greed that it engenders: slavery, subjection of others, hardening of hearts, refusal to share, fraud, theft. . . . Greed makes an idol of money and turns human beings into slaves. But poverty of spirit turns money into a source of sharing and sets human beings free.

"Store up treasures in heaven," says Jesus; "where your treasure is, there also will your heart be" (Matt 6:20-21). The Christian community received this warning from the Lord:

"No man can serve two masters.
He will either hate one and love the other,
or be devoted to one and despise the other.
You cannot serve God and mammon" (Matt 6:24).

St. Paul attributes the temptation to steal to laziness. The Christian who steals is going back to the life he or she led before conversion. "The thief must no longer steal, but rather labor, doing honest work with his own hands, so that he may have something to share with one in need" (Eph 4:28). In the Christian outlook, work is useful in three ways: it prevents theft, promotes independence, and makes sharing possible.

Just as sexual covetousness is not only what lurks in our hearts but also what we provoke, coveting the goods of someone else is also what we provoke when we flaunt our wealth in front of the poor, with whom we refuse to share our goods and our time. Selfishness makes us responsible when we cause others to covet. Sharing frees us from selfishness and covetousness.

At the root of every injustice is greed. Paul always groups greed, idolatry, and fornication together in order to portray the pre-Christian period of the first generation of converts (Rom 1:18-32). Greed is a form of idolatry: it easily leads to a denial of the true God and to being a slave to money. This is symbolic of paganism. Being without charity, the pagan, i.e., the Christian who reverts to his or her preconver-

Are money and wealth evil?

The temptation to steal

Didn't Christ deliver us from the pagan condition?

sion condition, uses others as tools for profit, without considering their rights; rather, having become a Christian, the believer should place him- or herself at the service of others. If, then, baptized persons lapse into greed, they lapse into the very pagan condition that Christ delivered them from.

Hasn't God's love been poured into our hearts?

Greed or covetousness is a direct attack on charity. It leads not only to idolizing money; it also leads to fornication, another pagan practice that prevailed before Christian conversion (Eph 5:3). Fornication debases one's neighbor. Those who serve money do not just use their neighbor for profit, they finish by taking advantage of the other person for their own pleasure. As in Paul's day, these three vices, which characterized the pre-Christian period of the baptized, continue to tempt today's Christians. By virtue of this, we must change our attitude day by day and, like new converts, allow ourselves to be filled with charity, for it is charity that enables us to clearly see where the benefit lies for our neighbor.

The tenth commandment sums up all the others by interiorizing them: may our heart of stone become a heart of flesh! Only those who love their neighbor as themselves can attain the purity of heart demanded especially by the two last commandments. Through love we identify the need of our neighbor: it is the *Law* in its entirety (Rom 13:8-10)! The joy that is felt by giving of oneself and in sharing has its source in God, whose generosity is overflowing:

Purity of heart, source of grace and abundance

"Whoever sows sparingly will also reap sparingly, and whoever sows bountifully will also reap bountifully. . . . God is able to make every grace abundant for you, so that in all things . . . you may have an abundance for every good work. . . . You are being enriched in every way for all generosity . . . ." (2 Cor 9:6, 8, 11).

"Happy are they . . . who walk in the law of the Lord."
(Ps 119, antiphon)

"Happy the men whose strength you are!
Their hearts are set upon the pilgrimage."
(Ps. 84:6)

211

Toward the Fullness of Life

"Your Father, who sees what is hidden, will repay you . . ."

Again, in the Beatitudes, Jesus calls upon us to live the law in the spirit of the gospel. He invites us to act "in secret" in the case of almsgiving, prayer, and fasting: to act in secret and not to be seen by people means that in all our conduct it is God whom we seek and love.

"But when you give alms, do not let your left hand know what your right is doing, so that your almsgiving may be secret. And your Father who sees in secret will repay you. . . . But when you pray go to your inner room, close the door, and pray to your Father in secret. And your Father who sees in secret will repay you. . . . When you fast, do not look gloomy like the hypocrites. They neglect their appearance, so that they may appear to others to be fasting . . . But when you fast, anoint your head and wash your face so that you may not appear to be fasting, except to your Father who is hidden. And your Father who sees what is hidden will repay you" (Matt 6:3-4, 6, 16-18).

The call of Jesus to share, to pray, and to fast establishes a threefold relationship: toward others, toward God, and toward ourselves. Prudence, as an attitude of heart, should make us open to community, as men and women of prayer, and moderate in our use of society's goods.

Being true and radiant

Being a Christian means being a witness. "You are the salt of the earth . . . and the light of the world," Jesus tells us. But he adds: "Your light must shine before others, that they may see your good deeds and glorify your heavenly Father" (Matt 5:13-16). Our witness has no meaning if it serves to glorify ourselves. Even if people don't acknowledge our faith and conduct, the fact that God sees us in secret makes us joyful and serene. Even more, says Jesus, "Blessed are you when they insult you and persecute you and utter every kind of evil against you [falsely] because of me. Rejoice and be glad, for your reward will be great in heaven" (Matt 5:11-12). Knowing that God looks upon us with love and love alone is sufficient to free us from wanting to be recognized and to compete.

213

That our Father sees in secret means that he sees everything. God's gaze is in no way disturbing, except for the one who desperately wants to withdraw from it. After having broken his relationship with God, Adam became afraid and hid himself (Gen 3:9). But God looks upon us as a physician looks upon a sick person—to help. Thus when Peter denied Jesus, "the Lord turned and looked at Peter" (Luke 22:61) . . . "Lord, you know everything; you know that I love you," said Peter (John 21:17).

The Father notices even the smallest instance of helping the poor. He listens attentively to our stammering prayer. He sustains and encourages our slightest effort at fasting and renunciation, he helps us to remain free people, and he continues to grant us our freedom of conscience.

"So be perfect, just as your heavenly Father is perfect"

Who among us has become the child of our mother's dreams? Human and moral perfection is gained by self-mastery and by acquiring virtues. To advance toward perfection is truly a great undertaking, but Christians do not subscribe to the theory that they can become perfect by themselves.

Is it possible to be perfect?

Christian perfection is a most singular thing. It is a gift of God. It is within everyone's reach, particularly of sinners! It consists of *loving with the Love with which we are loved.* This is why the Lord says, "Come to me, all you who labor and are burdened, and I will give you rest . . . my yoke is easy, and my burden light" (Matt 11:28, 30).

". . . as your heavenly Father is perfect" (Matt 5:48)

What some consider burdensome is human observance of the Law. But the yoke of the Lord is light because no one can say that it is burdensome to love, even if it demands much. Christian perfection consists of living in God's grace, God who knows our needs, our troubles, and our weaknesses, and who never abandons his creature. It is God who makes the difference in our lives, even to those who live on a high moral level.

God is perfect in himself, and his limitless love manifests itself through his mercy toward all human beings. "He makes his sun rise on the bad and the good, and causes rain to fall on the just and the unjust" (Matt 5:45). Like the father in the parable, he keeps watch for the return of the prodigal son. He offers his mercy to sinners and strives to have the elder son—who believes himself to be just—to share in the joy of the rediscovery (Luke 15:11-31). The Father comes forth to meet us by giving us his Son.

The call of all Christians to holiness stems from our membership in the Church that Christ has loved as his Bride: he has given his life for her in order to sanctify her (Eph 5:26-27), and he has filled her with his Holy Spirit.

"This is the will of God, your holiness" (1 Thess 4:3).

The sacramental life, especially sharing in the Eucharist, unites us to Christ and his Church. The Holy Spirit gives to each person a proper place and role in the Body of Christ. This is why the gifts that we have received are so varied. They correspond to the diversity of members who contribute to the harmony of this Body. Whether laypeople, reli-

215

gious, or members of the hierarchy, we joyfully admit that while we are not all called to the same form of holiness, the demands of love and holiness are the same for all.

We do not receive the various gifts that we have been given as individuals, but as members of a people. Thanks to these gifts, we share in the dynamism of the entire Church, in heaven and on earth; we act in community with our sisters and brothers, those who walk with us, those who after their death are being purified, and those who have entered into the glory of the Lord.

". . . the glorious freedom of the children of God" (Rom 8:21)

The Kingdom of God is the most precious good we can desire. It is worth more than everything that we own, as the parable of the treasure hidden in a field makes clear; the man who had discovered this treasure hid it again and, rejoicing at his find, went and sold all he had and bought that field (Matt 13:44). The Kingdom of God presupposes a great renunciation. Everything I have loved until now has no value when compared with the newness that the Kingdom brings. The habits and lifestyle I was attached to no longer limit me. I am free to discover my own way of living the gospel, beginning with the dynamism of the Spirit who dwells in me. This freedom has given us a Francis of Assisi, a Thomas More, a Catherine of Siena, a Teresa of Avila, and so many men and women who now radiate the newness of the gospel.

The powerful means of prayer (Matt 5:44)

"Love your enemies . . ." (Matt 5:44). Who can live out this strange call? The gospel summons is so boundless that it brings a feeling of joy to the human heart, but it is a joy

216

mixed with wonder. The disciples were so stunned by Jesus' teaching that they asked, "Who, then, can be saved?" Jesus looked upon them with love and said, "For human beings this is impossible, but for God all things are possible" (Matt 19:26).

One who wants to love God knows that it is the Father who calls and draws us to himself. The Father's kindness surpasses anything we can imagine:

"If you, then, who are wicked, know how to give good gifts to your children, how much more will the Father in heaven give the holy Spirit to those who ask him" (Luke 11:13).

As the Lord has taught us, we dare to say:

"Lord, teach us to pray . . ." (Luke 11:1).

Our Father
who art in heaven
hallowed be thy name,
thy kingdom come,
thy will be done,
on earth as it is in heaven.
Give us this day
our daily bread,
and forgive us our trespasses
as we forgive those
who trespass against us.
And lead us not into temptation
but deliver us from evil.

"Our Father"—This is how we call you, in both joy and trial, as your Son has taught us. You are our Father, for you

have made us your children, and you enable us to live as brothers and sisters.

"Our Father, who art in heaven"—With the Son and the Holy Spirit, you dwell in the heart of the person who receives you. Your dwelling is in heaven and you call us to your perfection that surpasses us.

"Hallowed be thy name"—Your name bespeaks your presence: may it be praised by sanctified hearts. May it be manifested to the world by your saints, known and unknown.

"Thy kingdom come"—Let your love and your justice reign in us and in the world. May your final Kingdom come, when the Son of Man comes on the day of resurrection of all men and women.

"Thy will be done"—Not ours but yours, with love and joy. Let it be done *"on earth as it is in heaven,"* as by the angels and saints who live in your presence and who intercede for us. Let it be done on earth, with the grace of your Holy Spirit, with the simplicity of Mary and the courage of the martyrs.

"Ask and you will receive . . ." (John 16:24).

"Give us this day our daily bread"—since we live by bread: the bread that you give us, *"fruit of the earth and the work of human hands"*; the bread of your Word that nourishes human beings even in the desert of loneliness and suffering; the *"living Bread"* of the Eucharist, your Son, the conqueror of death: "Whoever eats this bread will live forever" (John 6:58). Let us learn to share with those who hunger for bread and love *"so that they might have life abundantly."*

"But if you do not forgive others, neither will your Father forgive you" (Matt 6:15).

"Forgive us our trespasses"—for the sin that brought your Son to his death alienates us from you, personally and collectively. Forgive us through your Son who reconciles us with you. Make of us persons who forgive: enable us to be reconciled with you *"as we forgive those who trespass against us."*

"And lead us not into temptation"—Through your Son you have vanquished evil and suffering. Let all temptation find us vigilant; may every trial, rather than overcome us, strengthen us in the faith, in the love of our brothers and sisters, and in the hope against all hope.

218

"But deliver us from evil"—even if we have renounced evil and Satan, without you we are still unable to do anything either for ourselves or for our brethren.

"For thine is the kingdom, and the power, and the glory now and forever!"—In you we find the assurance of our faith, the power of love, and the gift of hope. Yes, "Amen."